The Eleventh Corps Artillery at Gettysburg

The Papers of Major Thomas Ward Osborn
Chief of Artillery

Edited by
Herb S. Crumb

Edmonston Publishing, Inc.
Hamilton, NY

Copyright © 1991 by Edmonston Publishing, Inc.

All rights reserved. No part of this book may be reproduced in any form, mechanical, photographic or electronic, nor may it be stored, transmitted or otherwise copied in a retrieval system without the written permission of the publisher, except by a reviewer who may quote brief passages in a review.

"Experiences at the Battle of Gettysburg" is part of the journals of Thomas Ward Osborn in the Colgate University Library, Hamilton, NY.

Library of Congress Catalog Card Number: 91-70764

ISBN 0-9622393-2-1

Printed in the United States of America on pH neutral paper.

10 9 8 7 6 5 4 3 2 1

Design by Ellen Peletz

The Eleventh Corps Artillery at Gettysburg

*To Grandpa Tom
from Amy Barton
Christmas - 1991*

Thomas Ward Osborn c. 1870.
(Courtesy of the Library of Congress.)

To Gettysburg's "honored dead."

"They gave their today for our tomorrow."
*Inscription from the monument
to Otsego County war veterans,
Cooperstown, NY*

Contents

Foreword by Gabor S. Boritt ix
Introduction xi
Letters to Abraham and Spencer Osborn 1
Experiences at the Battle of Gettysburg 7
Appendices
    Appendix A. Osborn's Battle Report
        from the Official Records.. 51
    Appendix B. *Philadelphia Weekly Times* Article 58
    Appendix C. McCartney's Report
        from the Official Records 83
    Appendix D. Biographical Sketch
        of Thomas Ward Osborn.......................................85
References 87
Index. 89

Illustrations and Maps

Illustrations

Thomas Ward Osborn, c.1870 ii
Eleventh Corps Artillery Plaque 6
View of Oak Hill from Dilger's Position 11
Lt. Wilkeson & Battery G, Fourth U.S. Artillery 12
Baltimore Pike Looking North Toward Gettysburg. 14
Route of Hay's Assault on East Cemetery Hill 28
Taft's Section Near the Gatehouse 33
Benner's Hill from Taft's Position 35
The Artillery in the Cemetery 41
Evergreen Cemetery Gatehouse, 1863 46

Maps

Eleventh Corps Artillery Positions, July 1, 1863 20
The Cemetery Hill Salient, July 2 & 3, 1863 30
    Inset: July 3, 1863; 3 p.m.

Foreword

Gettysburg is the mythological center of the American Civil War and ever shall remain that. Yet Gettysburg is also a very real and crucial turning point in that War. It is not surprising then that a mere listing of writings about the Battle fills a book. It may be a little more surprising, at least to the lay public, that, as the years go by, worthwhile additions to that large bibliography continue to be made. We learn to see old stories in new light. We discover events long forgotten. We learn to know individuals barely noticed in earlier histories, yet worth knowing.

At Gettysburg, Major Thomas Ward Osborn, the Chief of Artillery for Major General Oliver Otis Howard's Eleventh Corps, was one such individual. Stationed on Cemetery Hill, Osborn played an important and heroic role in the Battle. His accounts of that role, brought together for the first time by historian Herb Crumb, provide a valuable resource for the students of Gettysburg and the War.

We see the broken wheel of a cannon changed on the main street of Gettysburg, under fire, while Osborn's battery is escaping from pursuing Confederates. We hear a young officer ordered up front and saying, "in fifteen minutes I will be dead." And he is. Osborn takes stands on the Meade-Sickles controversy, as well as on the question of whether the Army of the Potomac pursued Lee with sufficient vigor after the Battle. And he repeats his claim that the idea to precipitate Pickett's Charge, by silencing the Union artillery, originated with him and was conveyed to Brigadier General Henry J. Hunt, the Chief of the Artillery for the Army. Hunt in his report took credit for himself, as did General

Meade before the Congressional Committee on the Conduct of the War. Alas, we poor humans.

A shell explodes under Osborn's horse and that of another officer on Cemetery Hill on the afternoon of July 3. The two are in conference. Almost miraculously neither is injured. Neither flinches. Yet Osborn recalls, with chagrin, that he looked down at the spot where the shell hit. The other officer did not. Many years later the artillerist of Cemetery Hill is still chagrined. Oh, ye soldiers of the American Civil War.

Spring, 1991 Gabor S. Boritt
Farm by the Ford Director of the
Gettysburg, PA Gettysburg Civil War Institute

Introduction

For our best understanding of the war we turn not to the multitude of latter-day interpretations, but to the past itself.

Richard B. Harwell
The War They Fought

One week after Gettysburg, 30 year old Major Thomas Ward Osborn wrote, "My command fights well." One month earlier, upon his appointment to command of the Eleventh Corps Artillery, he had described these batteries as the "worst in the Army of the Potomac." Following the Union defeat at Chancellorsville and upon the urging of Henry Hunt, Chief of Union Artillery, Hooker had ordered a reorganization of the Union batteries providing each army corps with its own artillery brigade. Osborn joined his new batteries on June 3rd. Included as a prelude to "Experiences at the Battle of Gettysburg" are the four letters to his two brothers, in which he describes his efforts to make these five batteries more efficient, efforts that one month later proved to have been successful.

Osborn had gained the attention of his commanding officer, Colonel Charles Wainwright, in his first action at Williamsburg, when the members of his Battery D, First NY Light Artillery volunteered to serve the guns of a regular U.S. battery, whose members had fled in the face of Confederate fire. Promoted to command the batteries of Berry's Third Corps division before Chancellorsville, his command helped there to stem the high tide of Jackson's flank assault. Following this able performance and upon the recommendation of Wainwright, he was promoted to major.[1]

Mustered into service in September, 1861 as a volunteer officer with no prior military experience, Lieutenant Osborn seemed to be an unlikely prospect for early promotion. There was little evidence to suggest the distinguished career that awaited him. Osborn recalled his recruitment of Battery D, later known as Winslow's battery, in remarks made at the dedication of its monument in the Wheatfield on July 2, 1888. His account reveals him as a decisive, no-nonsense and take-charge sort of young man, and, in retrospect, suggests that he was no ordinary civilian turned soldier.

"From August, 1860, to September, 1861, I was a law student in the office of Starbuck & Sawyer, Watertown, Jefferson County, N.Y. My home was in North Wilna, in the same county. Before, and until danger threatened, and after the breaking out of the war, I had no thought or intention of entering the military service. I took no interest whatever in military affairs, or in the military organizations then forming. The service had no charm for me, but the opposite. It was repulsive. This sentiment in no way changed until the battle of Bull Run had been fought and lost. Then, from a sense of duty alone, I determined to enter the army. I was not alone in this sentiment. Thousands of men shared it with me.

"I was a farmer's son, and a law student. I was without political or other controlling influences to aid me. Regiments, battalions, and companies were being organized all around me; but they were all of them under the patronage, supervision, and control of men of State or local prominence. All of these organizations, too, were indorsed and aided by powerful committees of citizens, who exerted themselves to their utmost to aid the enlisting officers to secure the men required in each respective command. It was everywhere said and generally conceded, that no man should organize even a company who was not sufficiently prominent to enable a committee of citizens to indorse him, and whose own personality should be a guarantee that the men whom he might enlist would have superior care and opportunities.

"I was not able to answer all these requirements; nor had I a county committee of influential men to vouch for and aid me. I had no knowledge of military affairs or organizations, or even of the several branches or arms of the service. I gave a few days to examining the subject from such sources as I could command, and with the trifling information so acquired, determined to seek admission into the artillery arm of the army. To accomplish this I must enlist a company. This I determined to do. Until my plans were fully, though crudely, matured, I consulted no one, nor did any person know that I contemplated entering the army. When, however, my plans were matured, I laid them before Mr. Sawyer.

"Mr. Sawyer then informed me that his personal friend, Lieut. Guilford D. Bailey, of the regular army, had been authorized to organize a regiment of light batteries, of which he was to be commissioned colonel. This was the first I had ever heard of Lieutenant Bailey, or of the proposed regiment of light batteries. Mr. Sawyer at once wrote to Lieutenant Bailey, inquiring if a company I might enlist would be received into his regiment. He replied that it would. I then undertook to enlist the necessary men.

"I required 100 men, and to secure them I had my personal efforts alone to depend upon. I returned to the farm and gave out that I intended to enter the army, and desired to enlist men sufficient for a company. Taking one of my brother's horses I rode on horseback over a large portion of Jefferson, Lewis, and St. Lawrence Counties. Whenever I heard of a man who had expressed a desire to enter the army, or who his neighbors thought might be induced to do so, I saw him and told him I was going into the service and asked him to go with me. I employed no other argument. I said nothing about the right or wrong of the controversy. I assumed every man knew as much about that as I did. I held out no special inducements for him to enlist. I told every man who were to be the officers of the company, so far as had been determined.

"While making this canvass for men I called on George B. Winslow, of Gouverneur, then a hardware merchant, with whom I had previously been acquainted. I laid my plans, and the results so far attained before him. He joined me in recruiting men. In the end, I had secured about sixty and he about forty men. On the 20th of August I reported to Colonel Bailey that I had secured the complement of men; on the 25th the men reported to me at Watertown; and on the 28th the company left Watertown for the recruiting rendezvous at Elmira, where we arrived on the 4th of September. Not one man who had signed the roll was missing. Being the fourth company arriving at the barracks it was designated as 'Company D.'"[2]

An 1860 graduate of Madison University (now Colgate University) in Hamilton, N.Y., he, like Wainwright, kept a journal of his wartime activities and this, along with numerous letters to his two brothers, Abraham (ACO) and Spencer C. Osborn (SCO), both St. Louis ministers, and other papers are in the Colgate archives. A portion of his journal was published in 1987 as *The Fiery Trail*. This work, edited by Richard Harwell and Philip Racine, introduced readers to Osborn and that portion of his journal and letters that covered his activities as Chief of Artillery of the Army of the Tennessee in a day-by-day description of Sherman's march through Georgia and the Carolinas. Understandably, Osborn found no time to make journal entries during the three days at Gettysburg, fighting which he described as the "severest battle of the war." There was his article dealing with Gettysburg published in the *Philadelphia Weekly Times* on May 31, 1879, and his report in the Official Records, both included as appendices to this more informal and personal account of incidents which he termed "worth remembering," and which he titled, "Experiences at the Battle of Gettysburg."

His recall of names is imperfect, mistakenly identifying Wilkeson as "Livingston." There is some confusion surrounding the events of the First Day, the location of the First Corps, the time of its withdrawal to Cemetery Hill, and other events that were beyond his immediate view. Nevertheless, his encounters with Meade, Howard, Hunt and other officers are revealing, and the personal anecdotes add to Gettysburg lore. His perception of the field as seen from Cemetery Hill gives the reader a less familiar view of the battle.

"Experiences at the Battle of Gettysburg" was probably written later than 1880, sometime after the publication of Henry Hunt's three part series in *Century Magazine* in 1886-87. Osborn may have felt slighted by his commanding officer's failure to mention that he, Osborn, at least shared the notion that a cessation of Union fire during the cannonade preceding Longstreet's assault on the Third Day would entice the Confederate infantry to attack. On the morning of the Second Day Osborn takes credit for being the first to note the gap between the First and Twelfth Corps positions on Culp's Hill. Perhaps he felt the Eleventh Corps batteries had shared unfairly in the criticism aimed at the Eleventh Corps infantry. He may have been seeking to gain some belated accolades for the Eleventh Corps artillery and/or to enhance the reputation of O.O.

Howard, his corps commander and personal friend. Pride in his brigade seems also to have been a motivating factor for writing this later account of the three days at Gettysburg.

Writing apparently without notes from imperfect memory, his narrative, written 25 years later, suffers apparent inaccuracies. When he ignores his resolve stated in the 1879 *Philadelphia Weekly Times* article "to deal with little. . .except the part borne by the artillery in position on Cemetery Hill," his account wanders and becomes something less than a vivid, firsthand history. Osborn certainly intended that his story be published much sooner than 100 years later.

Placed in an indefensible position north of town with both flanks open to attack, the Eleventh Corps faced inevitable defeat. Sometimes overlooked was the performance of Dilger's and Wheeler's batteries whose leapfrog team tactics and accurate fire had a deadly impact on Page's and Reese's Confederate batteries firing from Oak Hill. The rearguard action of the four Eleventh Corps batteries and their escape through the Gettysburg streets choked by the slower moving infantry probably prevented the mass surrender of Schurz's two divisions. Following their narrow escape, three of the batteries joined Wiedrich's battery on Cemetery Hill to continue the struggle.[3] On the Second Day with reinforcements from the Artillery Reserve, Osborn's command countered A.P. Hill's batteries north of town and joined Wainwright's First Corps batteries in silencing Ewell's artillery fire from Benner's Hill. On the Third Day, when caught in an enfilading fire from the same direction, his batteries silenced the short-lived destructive fire of Ewell's guns. The Eleventh Corps batteries, firing from Cemetery Hill, enfiladed the left flank of Pettigrew's division and certainly contributed to the disintegration and early retreat of Brockenbrough's brigade.[4] Wheeler's battery of Osborn's brigade joined the other Union artillery near the Angle to help in the repulse of Pickett.[5]

Like an unfinished giant jigsaw puzzle our picture of Gettysburg remains incomplete. The thousands of participants who left no written account of the battle are unable to fill in the missing pieces. Osborn's account furnishes another small piece to that puzzle. The significance of "Experiences at the Battle of Gettysburg" lies not in what it contributes to an understanding of the First Day's events, but rather in its description of the important and frequently overlooked role played by Osborn's batteries on the Second and Third Days. Few of the accounts of the final climactic Confederate assault of the Third Day have been written from the Cemetery Hill vantage point. Yet, Cemetery Hill was the center and key to the Union position, a high point that provided an excellent artillery site and observation post with an unobstructed view of the Confederate line on Seminary Ridge.[6] The Confederate attack upon East Cemetery Hill on the late evening of July 2nd posed a grave threat to Meade's position, and the hand-to-hand struggle that swirled around the batteries of Wiedrich and Ricketts was as desperate and deadly as that on the following day at the Angle.

The present day visitor to Cemetery Hill is denied the 1863 view enjoyed by Osborn. An open area and no-man's land separated the Union line on Cemetery Hill from Confederate positions in the town. Terrain features readily apparent during the battle have been lost to the commercial-residential sprawl and tree growth that surround the hill today. It is nearly impossible to trace the Eleventh Corps line on the western side of the Cemetery. The Visitors Center and adjacent parking lots intersect and cover the point at which that line met Robinson's First Corps division near Ziegler's Grove. Except for Dilger and one battery on his extreme left flank, Osborn's guns were located on the crest of Evergreen Cemetery, among the gravestones on the south side of the present day fence that separates the National Cemetery from Evergreen. Today, the National Cemetery is the dominant feature of Cemetery Hill and captures the visitor's attention. In a sense, this is appropriate in that it reminds the visitor that Civil War battlefields are memorials to the men who suffered and died upon them. Osborn's brief memoir helps us recall that Cemetery Hill was not always such a safe and quiet place.

Osborn's handwritten manuscript has been printed with minor modifications in spelling, punctuation and syntax. Misspelled proper names appear one time, followed by their correct spelling within brackets, and thereafter as corrected. A few long and rambling sentences have been reorganized for clarity into shorter sentences.

The generous assistance of Carl Peterson of the Colgate University Library, Kathleen Georg Harrison, historian at the Gettysburg National Military Park, and Lauren Prievo, Carthage Village historian, in making this volume available to the Civil War student is gratefully acknowledged. Special thanks are due Louis Fischer, licensed Gettysburg Battlefield guide, good friend and faithful "stomper," who cheerfully walked and rewalked the ground hallowed by the men who manned the batteries among the gravestones. The present-day photographs were taken by Mr. Fischer.

Herb S. Crumb
Spring, 1991
Norwich, NY

Notes

[1] Wainwright, in his personal journals, described Osborn, in his first combat experience, as "slow, as I expected," but credits him with doing "capital service." Wainwright wrote, "I learned that there was a good deal more grit in him than I thought," after Osborn had, while under fire, retrieved a gun mired in the mud.

[2] One of six children, three sisters and two brothers, Osborn was survived only by Abraham (ACO), a Baptist clergyman and President of Benedict College in Columbia, SC. His birthplace at North Wilna, NY, near Carthage, is presently within the confines of the Ft. Drum Military Reservation. Osborn never married and is buried in Abraham's family burial plot in Hillside Cemetery, North Adams, MA. Abraham was also a Madison University graduate and later served as a Trustee of Colgate University from 1893-1916.

[3] In his official report, Hunt credits Dilger and Wheeler for their effective counter-battery fire in the contest with Carter's Confederate battalion firing from Oak Hill. Heckman's battery lost two guns while covering the retreat of the Eleventh Corps through Gettysburg, and was retired to the rear for the remainder of the action.

[4] Southern sources confirm the early disintegration of Pettigrew's left flank, Brockenbrough's brigade, as it came within range of the enfilade fire from Cemetery Hill.

[5] Wheeler arrived at the Angle in time to assist in the repulse of Pickett's division.

[6] Hunt stated in his battle report, "Cemetery Hill commanded the positions which could be occupied by the enemy to the north and northwest." It also protected the Baltimore Pike, the Union Army's principal supply artery. O.O. Howard, in his autobiography, described Cemetery Hill as an observation post from which, "We could better understand the situation from our side, for we had higher points of observation and could take in the field. There was no shrubbery then to obstruct our view." Howard remembered the site presently occupied by the Soldiers' Monument in the National Cemetery as the highest point on the hill. As Osborn points out, the Union Artillery in the cemetery also presented a very visible and inviting target for Confederate gunners.

Letters to Abraham and Spencer Osborn
June 11 - July 3, 1863

Headquarters
Artillery Brigade, 11. Corps
Stafford Court House, Va.
June 11, 1863

[To SCO] A few days ago I sent you a copy of a special order by which I was assigned to the command of the Artillery Brigade of the Eleventh Corps. I have been on duty with it since last Thursday [June 3].

You will recollect it was this corps which first broke at Chancellorsville. I am told I have been highly complimented in being assigned to this corps to reorganize its artillery, but to me it is an unpleasant job. I found the batteries in a most deplorable condition and in a state of complete demoralization. So far I have been in the saddle the most of everyday and taxing my ingenuity to determine how best to make the batteries serviceable again. So far I am succeeding well, but there is much to do yet. I left the best artillery in the army when I left the Third Corps, and when I came here I took the worst. If we lie still two or three months, I can put it in good shape. If we move soon, I do not see how it can be done. The officers are willing, but have never been subject to any discipline or military supervision whatever. All their military habits are excessively loose. I will do my best to bring these batteries up to a good standard of efficiency.

*Headquarters
Artillery Brigade, 11. Corps
Stafford Court House, Va.
June 11, 1863*

    [To ACO] My last letter to you was written from the Artillery Reserve of the army. Thursday morning of last week I was ordered to report to General Howard, Commanding the Eleventh Corps, as his Chief of Artillery. I soon found I had been assigned to perform a difficult task. The artillery of this corps has been known throughout the army as the worst in the army. I am told that my assignment here was a compliment. General Tyler remonstrated against the order transferring me from the Artillery Reserve, but General Hunt said he considered me equal to the work required and I must go. He said the batteries were worthless, and a disciplinarian and industrious officer was required. So I am here. I have nowhere seen anything to be compared to these batteries with the exception perhaps of Captain Dilger's battery. They have scarcely a resemblance to light batteries. Generals Hooker, Hunt and Howard have each assured me that I should have everything I wished to re-equip and get them into serviceable order. I have confidence in my ability to bring them out so, providing the army lies still a considerable time, as it will require quiet to accomplish much with and for them. These batteries have evidently never had a commander; that is, an officer who exercised any control over them.
    The first thing I did was to ride through the camps and look over the debris of what should be and once was light batteries. The next was to quietly but firmly let the captains know I commanded the artillery of this corps. A part of them were willing to accept the situation, and a part of them were not. I very soon stopped all foolishness by informing those who developed a disposition to be fractious that a disobedience of military orders would not be overlooked. One battery I have broken up and sent the men to Washington. The others I have inspected and had nearly every part of their material condemned, even going so far as to condemn the clothing the men had on. I have directed the officers of each battery to make requisition for a new outfit in place of material condemned. I have ordered them to change their camps to get them out of the reach of the refuse of the old camps. In every step I have taken, I have directed the officers to comply strictly with the requirements of the artillery tactics. I have

ordered them to drill certain hours of the day, and most assuredly they needed it. I have established my brigade Headquarters in the immediate vicinity of the batteries and have organized a brigade staff. Indeed, I have undertaken a complete and thorough reorganization of these batteries. I think by close attention and constant watching I can soon get them into fair condition and fit for the field. They are not so now.

Our cavalry crossed the Rappahannock River last Friday and are reported to have had a severe engagement, but I know little about it. The cavalry movement is said to have called General Lee's army back this way after it had gone towards Western Virginia.

Headquarters
Artillery Brigade, 11. Corps
Centerville, Va.
June 16, 1863

[To ACO] We left our camp at Stafford Court House between three and four o'clock on the 12th instant and marched 13 miles. The next day we made Catlett's Station, 20 miles, next day, Centerville, 20 miles, and tomorrow move again. I think now we are going toward Harpers Ferry. The army now is all here. You know as much of the enemy as I do.

Headquarters
Artillery Brigade, 11. Corps
Middletown, Md.
June 27, 1863

[To ACO] We reached here last evening and as we are in the advance we may be here all day for the army to close up. On the 25th this corps marched 27 miles. The enemy is reported to have left Boonsboro, 12 miles from here, yesterday, going north. The citizens estimate the force all the way from 20,000 to 60,000 men.

General Hooker's headquarters will reach here today. I have no idea how long we are to remain here, but probably only a day or two.

You ask me about the brigading of the artillery. After the

battle of Chancellorsville, General Hooker ordered a reorganization of the artillery. Each army corps was allowed a brigade of five batteries with a brigade staff and organization. Any surplus batteries beyond this allowance to the corps were sent to the Artillery Reserve of the army, there to be organized into brigades of seven batteries each and then into divisions of two brigades each. Brigadier General Tyler is to command the Artillery Reserve. The volunteer division to which I belonged is to be commanded by Major Tompkins of the Rhode Island Artillery, who ranks me by more than a year.

I have learned since I came here that after I had taken command of the brigade in the Artillery Reserve, General Howard applied to General Hooker for an artillery officer who could fit his batteries for the field. They were, by his own representations, very bad. After some hesitation General Hooker transferred me. I knew nothing of all this until I received the order assigning me as Chief of Artillery of the Eleventh Corps.

We are now in sight of the battlefield of South Mountain. I never saw a more beautiful country. It is nicely cultivated.

Headquarters
Artillery Brigade, 11. Corps
Gettysburg, Pa.
July 3, 1863

[To ACO] We have been fighting three days. This has been the severest battle of the war.

Editor's Note: *Four of the five batteries in Osborn's brigade had served with the Eleventh Corps at Chancellorsville. Wilkeson's Battery G, 4th U.S. Artillery joined Osborn's command after Chancellorsville. Captain Dieckman had commanded the 13th Independent New York Battery at Chancellorsville. Following Dieckman's promotion to major and transfer to the 15th New York Heavy Artillery, Lieutenant William Wheeler had been promoted to command the battery. The battery Osborn speaks of breaking up and sending back to Washington was Blenker's 2nd Independent New York Battery. It was mustered out on June 13,*

1863 and its three year men transferred to Wiedrich's Battery I, 1st New York. Wilkeson's battery was his replacement.

Osborn deserves considerable credit for the improved performance of the batteries at Gettysburg although Dilger had performed splendidly at Chancellorsville, his heroics there to eventually gain him a Congressional Medal of Honor. The war produced no finer artillery officer, North or South.

Osborn's harsh criticism of the Eleventh Corps batteries may have reflected some of the prejudice against "Germans" shared by the rank and file in the Union Army. His initial estimate of Dilger was certainly unfair and inaccurate.

Eleventh Corps Artillery Plaque on West Howard Avenue, Gettysburg, PA.

Experiences at the Battle of Gettysburg

This article was written several years ago, probably about 1880, as the writer's personal recollections of the Battle of Gettysburg and in it he has intentionally made frequent reference to himself. At the time it was written, it was mislaid and forgotten and accidentally found a few weeks since. It was not intended to be a history of the battle nor a description of the entire battle. But as the commander of a brigade of artillery, five batteries, much increased during the battle, he bore an active part in the fight. In those three days the incidents worth remembering were too many to write, but from them he has selected a few for this article. The writer's frequent use of the first person is to be understood in this sense. The batteries comprising his brigade were commanded by Captains Dilger, Heckman, Weidrick [Wiedrich], Wheeler and Lieutenant Livingston [Wilkeson].

At the time he was Chief of Artillery on the staff of General Howard and commanding the Eleventh Corps Artillery with the rank of Major. As the artillery of the army was then organized, the chief of artillery of a corps, whatever his grade might be, commanded the artillery of the corps, as a Brigadier General commanded a brigade of infantry, with the same or even greater independence of action.

The heavy work required of the artillery in that battle brought the writer into personal communication with many prominent and now historical characters, a few of whom are mentioned. While a battle is in progress, any one officer can see but an exceedingly small section of the field and what he sees and does may not be seen or known by another officer not fifty yards from him. For this reason personal recollections of the man are of interest and value and are as new and interesting to another veteran who served in the same army and fought in the same battles as to a civilian.

On the first of June, Hooker's and Lee's armies were both at Fredericksburg, Va. On June 6th, Lee drew out two of his three corps commanded respectively by Longstreet, Ewell and Hill, and moved them towards Culpeper. On the 9th, Ewell's and Longstreet's corps and Stewart's [Stuart's] cavalry were at Culpeper, and Hill still at Fredericksburg. On the 12th, Ewell was in the Shenandoah Valley, Longstreet at Culpeper, and Hill at Fredericksburg, as Hooker started the Third and First Corps toward Bealeton. On the 13th, one division of Ewell's corps had arrived at Martinsburg, Longstreet was north of Culpeper, and Hill left Fredericksburg. Hooker had moved his army up to cover Washington.

On the 17th, Lee's army was stretched along from Culpeper to the bank of the Potomac, and Hooker's army lay between Lee's army and Washington. On the 24th, Ewell was in Pennsylvania and Longstreet and Hill in Maryland. Hooker was still in Virginia near the Potomac River covering Washington. On the 28th, Lee's army was in Pennsylvania moving towards Harrisburg, and Hooker was in Maryland near and about Frederick.

On the 28th, Hooker was relieved from the command of the Army of the Potomac, and General Meade, then commanding the Fifth Corps, was assigned to its command. On the 29th, Meade was moving his army, still in Maryland, towards Gettysburg, and Lee, still in Pennsylvania, was drawing his army back towards Gettysburg on the 30th. Both armies were nearer Gettysburg, the First and Eleventh Corps having entered Pennsylvania and the remainder in Maryland. Lee's army was more compact, and he had a larger force near Gettysburg than Meade. Geographically, Lee was north of Gettysburg, and Meade was south of Gettysburg.

The writer has not at hand the exact force of the two armies. They were about equal and each had about 70,000 men.[1] The losses in killed, wounded and prisoners for the three days of fighting did not differ much in the two armies. Each lost between 20,000 and 25,000 men, or a total loss in the two armies between 40,000 and 50,000 men. The losses in Meade's army on the First and Second Days were probably greater than Lee's, and on the Third day, Lee's losses were much greater than Meade's. It is well enough to state, in this general way, the approximate numbers engaged and the approximate losses as preliminary to what follows.

The First Day

In the evening of June 30th, the Eleventh Corps camped at Emmitsburg. Early in the morning of July 1st, General Howard received information that General Reynolds, commanding the First and Eleventh Corps, was in the immediate neighborhood of the enemy near Gettysburg. He directed Howard to proceed with all possible speed to his support, which Howard did as he moved upon the direct road to Gettysburg. It was near noon when Howard was notified that there had been a serious collision between Lee's advance and the First Corps, that the corps had been checked and Reynolds killed. Upon Reynolds's death Howard assumed the command of the two corps. When Howard was notified of the change in command, he was at the head of the Eleventh Corps, four or five miles from Gettysburg. I, as Chief of Artillery, was with him at the time. Before going to the front, he gave a few hasty orders and directed me to order the batteries to hasten to the front and then to follow him. He at once rode rapidly to the front. General Doubleday, a division commander of the First Corps, was in command of the corps while Reynolds commanded the two corps, and Doubleday remained in command of the corps after Howard assumed the command of the two corps. Howard ordered General Schurz to assume command of the Eleventh Corps. General Schimmelfennig succeeded Schurz in command of his division. I rode back to the several batteries and gave them orders to proceed to the front as rapidly as possible. Two of them I passed up to the head of the column, or near it, and then joined Howard at the front.[2]

I rode through the town and found Howard in front of it on the road to the Lutheran Seminary, which the First Corps advanced upon and upon which Reynolds had been killed. When I arrived on the field, Howard was already withdrawing the First Corps from the front to secure the position of Cemetery and Culp's Hills in the rear of the town.[3] The enemy was crowding the corps hard, which was making a strong fight as it fell back in good order. It had already suffered severely and Reynolds was killed, but there was no demoralization. It had inflicted still greater loss upon the enemy, which was altogether too strong for it. When I arrived on the field, Captain Griffith, an aide of General Howard, had been killed while carrying orders to the front.

I had been with the General a few minutes when Wheeler's and Heckman's [Dilger's] batteries of my command arrived.[4] The artillery of the corps had been organized into a brigade only a short time previously. I had not before been in battle with the corps or seen any of these batteries under fire. I placed the two batteries on the left of the Seminary Road where Howard was, and at once opened fire to aid the infantry of the First Corps to withdraw. Howard ordered Schurz, with Barlow's and Schimmelfennig's divisions, through the town and to the right to check the advance of Ewell's corps, then approaching the town from the north, while he withdrew the First Corps. Steinwehr's division was retained on Cemetery Hill to entrench while the other troops were being withdrawn. After I had Wheeler's and Dilger's batteries well at work, I rode back to town and from there took Battery G, 4th U.S. Artillery, commanded by First Lieutenant Wilkeson, to the front with Schurz's command. Schurz went into position on the bluff independent of, and to the right of, Doubleday's command and intercepted Ewell's advance to the town and the rear of the First Corps. I put Wilkeson's battery into position and remained with it until it was well at work.[5]

Leaving Wilkeson, I rode quickly to Cemetery Hill to look after the position of Dilger's [Heckman's] and Wiedrich's batteries left on the Hill with Steinwehr's division, and from there again to Wheeler's and Dilger's batteries. I found them returning to the town in the retrograde movement with the First Corps from the front towards Seminary Ridge.[6] Wheeler had lost one gun; the carriage had been broken by a solid shot from the enemy's guns.

I again returned to Wilkeson's battery, where I met Wilkeson being carried to the rear by his men on a stretcher. One leg had been cut off at the knee by a cannon shot. He spoke to me and was cheerful and hopeful. I knew at a glance that the wound was fatal. There was no time for me to stop and, after talking with him, perhaps a quarter or half-minute, I left him. I never saw him again, as he died a few hours later. He was very young, less than twenty years of age, and of remarkable promise.

I soon hurried on to the front where I found the battery

View of Oak Hill from Dilger's Position.

Lt. Bayard Wilkeson and Battery G, Fourth U.S. Artillery.

engaged in line with Barlow's division. The lines of battle were in the open field and very close together. The enemy's line overlapped ours to a considerable extent on both flanks. Lieutenant Bancroft was in command of Wilkeson's battery and doing good work. I knew that the two divisions must soon fall back or would be drawn back. I gave Bancroft what instructions were necessary and returned to get the other four batteries into satisfactory positions. A few moments after I left the line, General Barlow was seriously wounded and fell into the hands of the enemy.

I again reached Wheeler's and Heckman's batteries just after they entered the town in their efforts to gain Cemetery Hill under Howard's instructions.[7] They were closely followed by the enemy who were within easy musket range of them along a straight street and were firing rapidly. I took personal command of the two batteries until they were in the middle of town where they could turn a corner and get out of the range of the musketry.

While on the straight street, by which the batteries entered the town, an accident occurred which brought out the cool and soldierly qualities of the men. The forewheel of one of the gun carriages broke and, of course, stopped the movement of that gun. I ordered the gunners to unlimber the gun and open fire to the rear with cannister and the remaining men to take the fifth wheel from a caisson and replace the broken one. All this took two or three minutes, but the cannister fire down the street to the rear so demoralized the enemy skirmishers following us that they ran into the yards, side streets and behind houses. They stopped their fire for a time sufficient to get on the extra wheel, limber up and again move on. For the men of that gun the case was quite desperate and most admirably managed.

The batteries moved to the center of the town on a street separate from our infantry. A considerable number of men were killed and wounded and some horses were lost, but all the guns and caissons were taken through the town. While retiring, the infantry could cover themselves to some extent with a rear guard, but the artillery could not at all protect itself and necessarily lost a larger percentage of men than did the infantry.

As Wheeler's and Heckman's batteries arrived on Cemetery Hill, Schurz was just arriving with his two divisions. The First Corps preceded the Eleventh and were already in position, mainly on Culp's Hill. Steinwehr's division had occupied the hill since its arrival and had done considerable labor in

View of Gettysburg and the Baltimore Pike, Looking North from Cemetery Hill. (*Courtesy of the Gettysburg National Military Park.*)

throwing up breastworks, but had not been engaged. The First Corps and the two divisions with Schurz of the Eleventh Corps came in. As Arrowsmith and I were talking, he received orders to move his regiment to the front and cover their withdrawal. As he received the order, he rose, gave me his hand and said, "Good-by, Osborn. In fifteen minutes I will be dead. Good-by and may you be successful." I made an easy reply and told him I had no fear of any such result. He replied, "You are mistaken. In fifteen minutes I will be dead." It was true. A few minutes later he was shot and instantly killed. This was the most remarkable premonition of death I knew of during the war. Arrowsmith was a young man of unusual promise.[8]

Upon arriving at Cemetery Hill, I found that Wheeler's and Heckman's batteries were very near the last of the troops to arrive, with the exception of a small body of troops of the First Corps. That corps was in or going into position along the crest of Culp's Hill or continuation of Cemetery Hill, but upon the opposite and right side of the Baltimore Pike. The lines of the two corps connected at the gate of the cemetery on the Pike. The two divisions that were with Schurz at the front and Bancroft's battery came upon Cemetery Hill ahead of Wheeler's and Heckman's batteries. Steinwehr's division had not moved from the position first taken.

Howard, in person and through his aides, located the two corps along the crests of Cemetery and Culp's Hills. Colonel Wainwright, Chief of Artillery of the First Corps, retained command of the First Corps batteries upon Culp's Hill, while I retained command of the Eleventh Corps batteries on Cemetery Hill. Howard gave me instructions in regard to placing the artillery, but expressed himself as being satisfied after I had put them into position in compliance with my own views. I think the same was true as to Wainwright's batteries as put into position by him.[9] The organization of the line, infantry and artillery, was for the purpose of resisting an assault from Lee.

The battles of the two following days proved that the placing of the batteries into position was as good as was possible. It was about five o'clock when the two corps were in position, and all the infantry were throwing up breastworks. After the day's fighting and heavy losses, the First Corps probably had 5,000 men and the Eleventh Corps about 8,000. I am not able to be exact about these figures. These two corps were the smallest in the army before the battle commenced, and that day they lost heavily. All told, I do not think there were more than 13,000 men in line that evening. Each corps had five light batteries. About half of Lee's army, or in the vicinity of 35,000 or 40,000 men, were facing us within artillery range and the picket lines were close together and keeping up an active fire.[10]

As I mentioned above, I had not been in battle with the Eleventh Corps before that day and had not before served under Howard in battle. Except what he had seen of me the preceding four or five hours, he knew nothing about me under trying circumstances. While the sun was still up and sufficient time existed for Lee to attack, Howard said to me, "Evidently, Lee's whole army is on our front, and he will attack yet this evening or early in the morning. I have no support in less than 20 miles. It is impossible for us to successfully withstand Lee, and we shall be wiped out of existence. I have determined to stay and fight to the last, with the view of crippling Lee's army as much as possible so that the remainder of the army, when it arrives, will be able to defeat him." After making this statement, he said, "There is no hope of our whipping Lee, but I intend to make the utmost fight I can. Will you stand by me to the end?" Of course, I said that I would do so.

That was my first fight with Howard, and we became better acquainted before the battle closed. I served with him to the end of the war and was in many battles with him, but he never after gave me an explicit order on a battlefield. I learned his plan and cooperated with him to the best of my ability and judgment, and fortunately without ever receiving a criticism for the work the artillery did.

Lee did not attack that evening nor early the next morning, and not until Meade had brought large reinforcements upon the field and our line was extended and strengthened. Meanwhile Lee's forces were coming into his line very rapidly, and every hour he was stronger than he was the preceding hour. So the experiment was not made to see how long a dozen thousand men could stand against from 40,000 to 60,000 of Lee's veterans before the twelve thousand were killed, wounded or captured.

After the battle opened in the morning, Lee urged his army in from all directions. In the evening it was vastly stronger than in the morning, and the next morning greatly stronger than in the evening. At no time during the war was I engaged in just such a battle as Howard prepared to fight. It was not to be a battle to gain a victory, but to cripple the enemy as much as possible. While we were being crushed, the other troops might win a victory after we were dead and the fight made over our dead bodies.

The immediate prospect was not in the nature of a jubilee, but I have no doubt that if Lee had attacked that evening or early the next morning, Howard would have made the fight precisely as he said, whatever might have come. That item of Howard's plans for the first night of Gettysburg has never before been committed to print, nor do I know whether at the time he gave to any other subordinate the information he gave me regarding this plan. In such a desperate encounter the artillery was necessarily an important factor, and as a commander of artillery, I was a comparative stranger to him. I do not know but that he gave all of his immediate subordinate commanders the same information regarding his plan.

Our wounded men in that first day's fight were left either on the field where they fell or in the town. In either case they were in the hands of the enemy and were prisoners, as we had fallen back through the town and left it in the possession of Lee's army. The night was an anxious one. There was but a handful of us in the immediate presence of a powerful enemy. That part was fully appreciated by many of us. In my own mind I knew that if Lee attacked, a most terrible struggle would follow on our part.

The first day's work had tired the troops and they slept well through the night, and the early morning found them rested and in good spirits and condition. At that early hour no reinforcements had arrived to strengthen us, but Lee did not attack. For him it was a lost opportunity. For us it was a blessing not very much disguised. At daylight we found the enemy's picket line and our own within easy musket range of each other, wrapped around the position of the First and Eleventh Corps in a semicircle and stretching off to the right and left indefinitely.

I should have said that the line of the two corps, as they occupied the ridge of Cemetery and Culp's Hills, were in the form of a crescent, as a new moon, with the arc to the north. The line did not take the horseshoe shape, of which so much has been written, until the flanks of these two corps were extended by the arrival of other corps.

A great deal has been said and written, at one time and another, about the selection of the Cemetery Hill and Ridge as the field of battle, in which there has been a good deal of truth and considerable fiction. It appears that when Buford with his cavalry command passed through Gettysburg, which lies in a wide pass in the mountain range, in the morning and brought on the first collision with Lee's troops, he pointed out the hill and ridge as a good defensive line. I am under the impression that Reynolds's attention was also attracted to it, but he preferred Seminary Ridge, which Lee occupied during the battle. The first fighting, that in which Reynolds was killed, was done in his effort to get possession of Seminary Ridge.[11] That ridge was a mile beyond the town, and there the First Corps had its First Day's fight. This also covered the pass. It was between one and two miles in advance of Cemetery Ridge and nearly parallel to it.

    The First Corps was being forced from Seminary Ridge when Howard arrived on the field, and his primary object was to find a position to which he could withdraw the First Corps. From the nature of the ground, there was no mistaking the best line for a man who was trained and experienced in war. Howard at once selected Cemetery Hill and its flanking ridges as the proper position to fall back to and establish his line of battle. He placed Steinwehr's division on the hill with instructions to entrench and to make a rallying point upon which to fall back. He sent Schurz beyond the town with two divisions to check Ewell's corps, which was approaching Gettysburg on its return from Harrisburg. All these troops Howard drew back and put into position on Cemetery and Culp's Hills. Other officers also noticed the advantages of the line for defensive battle before Howard occupied it, but Howard knew nothing of what other officers had said and done in the matter. Under the pressure of Lee's overwhelming force, independent of what all others had said or conclusions they had arrived at and without any knowledge of their views, he selected and occupied Cemetery Hill.[12]

    No civilian without military training would, before the battle was fought, have selected that ground as a superior battlefield upon which to fight a defensive battle. Cemetery Hill is a low elevation with an extension on the right, a low ragged range of hills with a well-defined crest stretching about three-quarters of a mile to Rocky [Rock] Creek. On the left of the hill, the ground fell off to a low swell from three or four to six feet high and sloping very gradually both ways from this ridge or swell. In fact, to the farmer's eye there would be no ridge at all but merely rolling ground on the face of the plain. This swell or ridge continued unbroken to Little Round Top, a mile and a half from Cemetery Hill. This low ridge made an excellent line, and with a line of breastworks thrown up along its highest elevation, made an almost impregnable position. The front of this line, at no point except near the extreme left, was so steep or rough that a line of battle could not move over it with perfect ease and without breaking step.

In the evening of the First Day Hancock arrived on the field and under Meade's orders assumed command at the front. Meade did not arrive until about midnight. After his arrival he was in command on the field.[13] Howard and Hancock resumed command of their corps, and Newton was assigned to the command of the First Corps.

Editor's note: *Written on 29 July 1863, Osborn's battle report contained in the Official Records is the most accurate account of the events involving his brigade on July 1st. He identifies his batteries accurately and confines his comments to the action in which he was directly involved. See Appendix A.*

Having followed the different routes to Gettysburg, his batteries arrived at different times. Dilger, attached to and in advance of Schurz's division, followed the Taneytown Road by way of Horner's Mill.

Dilger arrived before Osborn and was ordered north of town between the Carlisle and Mummasburg Roads by Schurz in support of the advance units of Schurz's division, the 45th N.Y. and the 61st Ohio, who deployed in a skirmish line and advanced up the slopes of Oak Hill. Wheeler, who arrived one half hour later with Steinwehr's division, was ordered to the support of Dilger by Osborn. Shortly after, Wilkeson arrived and was hurried to the support of Barlow's division on the Heidlersburg (Harrisburg) Road. Initially, Heckman remained in reserve with Wiedrich on Cemetery Hill to be hurried later to the support of Schurz's division now under Schimmelfennig's command. Wiedrich remained through July 3rd in the position initially assigned to his battery on Cemetery Hill.

Dilger and Osborn claim arrival at 10 a.m. Most sources set the time nearer noon or after. Schurz reported that his advance units arrived at 12:30 p.m. Civil War armies made little or no effort to standardize time or to synchronize watches, and each officer and man seems to have been his own timekeeper.

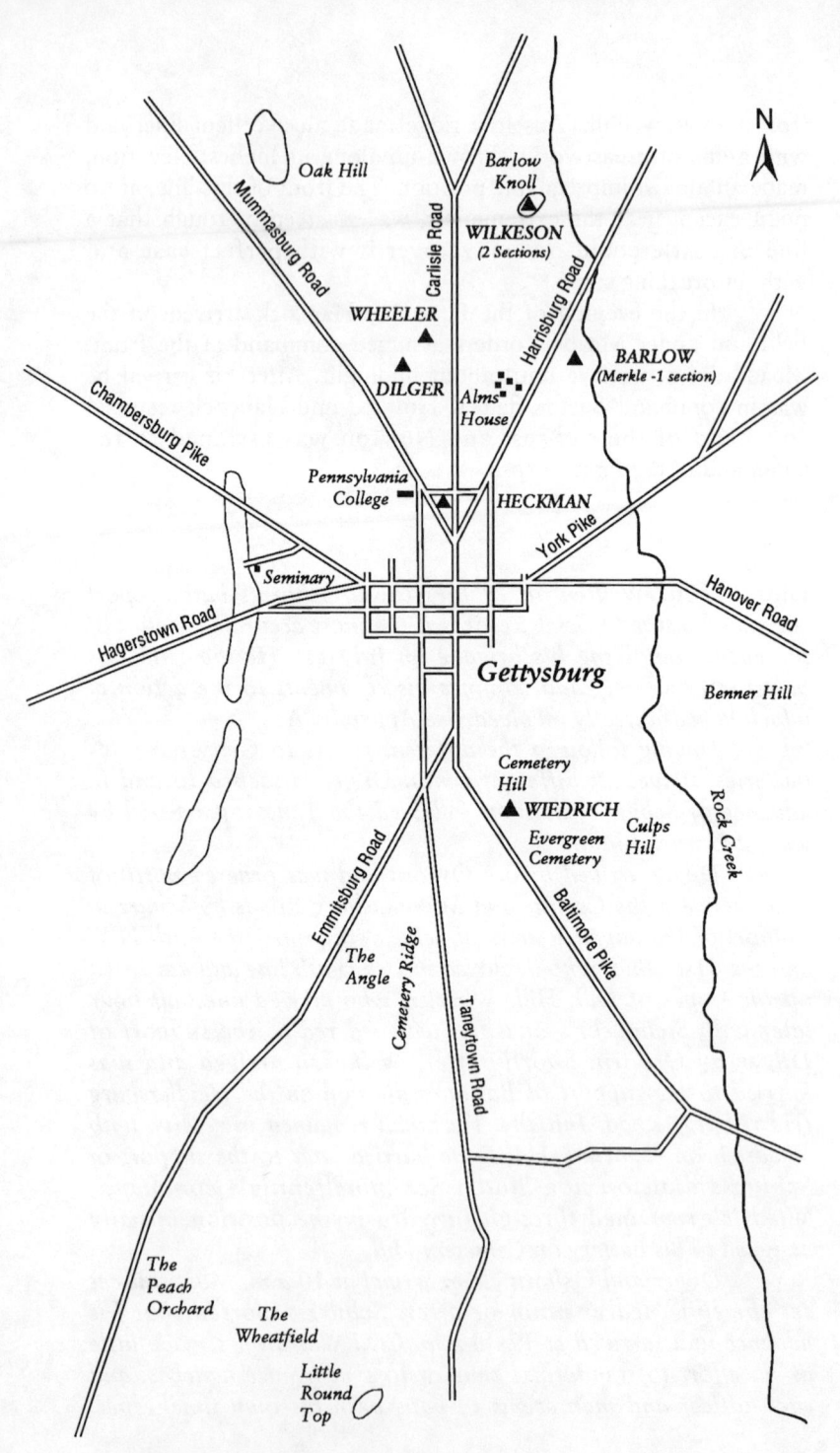

Eleventh Corps Artillery Positions, July 1, 1863

Given the shortage of sundials it is not surprising that estimated times of arrival and departure vary greatly. To describe an event as occurring "earlier" or "later than," or "before" or "after" an established event proves to be a more reliable method for measuring time.

Osborn's batteries arrived at different times and were widely separated during the engagement. Subsequent withdrawal through Gettysburg made it most difficult for him to exercise control of the separated units. His accounts reflect some of the confusion attending these circumstances. Osborn was faced with the almost impossible task of describing a two or three hour period in which the Eleventh Corps batteries found themselves in a constantly changing situation in which chaos and confusion were the norm.

The Second Day

As soon as it was light enough to see in the morning of the Second Day, I made an inspection of the line in the rear of Cemetery Hill to learn as far as I could what there was in that locality. The picket line covered the rear. I could not pass that, but I could go far enough to get a very clear idea of the general character of the field in that direction.

Just at the rear of the cemetery there were several open fields. At the farther side of the open fields and a little beyond the right flank of the First Corps, there was a break in the hills through which Rock Creek ran. This was about three-fourths of a mile from the cemetery. This break made an easy passage through the range of hills for Lee's army and was covered only by a thin picket line. It occurred to me that when Lee again attacked that his troops would come through the passage in the hills. A body of troops could go through without difficulty. This would have placed them directly in the rear of the First and Eleventh Corps. As I found the pass early in the morning, Ewell's corps could have moved through at a right shoulder shift and with another of Lee's corps in front, our two corps would have been completely surrounded with a stronger force both in front and rear.[14]

I reported these facts and my conclusions to Howard and suggested that a force should be sent to hold the pass. He said that he had no troops to spare, not even one regiment, and he could not occupy it.

    I then told him that I thought it was necessary that the pass should be guarded, and if he would give me permission, I would hold it with artillery until he could change front with the infantry to receive an attack. With the General's approval I withdrew two batteries from Cemetery Hill, separated them into sections of two guns each and put them into position. These ten guns, spreading over a front of more than half a mile, could bring a converging fire upon the head of a column coming through the narrow pass along the bank of Rock Creek. This fire if it had been necessary to employ it, would have checked any column long enough for the General to swing a division of troops around to meet the movement. He could probably have held such a movement by Ewell back until he was reinforced by other troops which were then approaching the field. I directed the battery commanders that, if they discovered a movement through the pass, to open upon the head of the column and hold it until relieved by the infantry. Later in the day that identical movement was made by Ewell's corps, but not until the Twelfth Corps, commanded by General Slocum, had arrived and occupied the pass.[15]

    After sunrise, General Hunt, Chief of Artillery of the Army, rode upon the hill and asked me to ride around to the batteries with him. While we were riding along the line of the hill, he noticed the batteries on the plain and turning to me abruptly, he said with decided emphasis, "What are those batteries doing there?" I told him that the pass was not guarded and that those batteries were all the protection the army had to prevent its being turned. To this he said, "Batteries should not be so exposed without support." I informed him that the General had no troops to spare to support them. He then asked, "Whose plan was it in putting them there?" I told him that I had reconnoitered the pass, found it open and had volunteered to General Howard to guard it with two batteries. After completing his inspection, he was about to ride off when I asked him what instructions he had to give. He replied, "None."

    He then told me that he would leave instructions with the Reserve Artillery to furnish me with any batteries or whatever ammunition I might call for and then rode off. The batteries were not withdrawn until the Twelfth Corps arrived and occupied the pass. These were the exact facts in regard to placing these batteries, a little after daylight, in position to guard the pass of

Rock Creek. I notice that General Hunt in his *Century Magazine* article on the Battle of Gettysburg says that he placed them there and assumes all the credit. He had nothing whatever to do with placing them there as they were in position from a half hour to an hour before he saw them. All he did was not to give orders for their withdrawal.

In the afternoon, Lee made a desperate effort to force the pass with Ewell's corps. He was repulsed. Lee postponed the attempt to break through by the pass of Rock Creek eight hours too long. If he had made the effort in the early morning with the same force he used in the afternoon, there would have been nothing but those ten guns to have disputed the passage until Howard had changed front with part of his command and weakened his front line. However, this last comment applies to all parts of the field in the morning. Until about ten o'clock there was nothing to resist Lee except the little handful of men on Cemetery and Culp's Hills.

The operations of the Second Day of the battle did not bring the Eleventh and First Corps into severe fighting until between sunset and dark. The several corps which were absent the First Day were ordered to Gettysburg, and by marching most of the night and the morning, they arrived in the forenoon. About noon of the Second Day the line was extended from the right of Howard's command to occupy Rock Creek and on the left toward Little Round Top.

The severely contested battle on the extreme left was brought about by Longstreet moving to attack Meade's left and encountering the Third Corps commanded by General Sickles as it was going into position. This fight involved Longstreet's and part of Hill's corps of Lee's army and Sickles's, Sykes's, Hancock's and part of Slocum's corps of Meade's army. It was a desperately fought engagement and Longstreet forced Sickles's line back from half to three-quarters of a mile. However, the line in its retired position was stronger than in the advanced position. Lee's forces suffered as much as Meade's did in that fight, and before night their attacks gave out. It was a drawn battle. As the Eleventh Corps was not engaged in that part of the field and we were not attacked until later in the evening, I will not speak more at length upon it.

There was one item connected with Sickles's fight in which I feel an honest pride and therefore will be excused for speaking of it, though I saw but little of the battle fought by

Sickles. I took into the service, as its Captain, Battery D, First New York Light Artillery. The company was composed of Jefferson, Saint Lawrence and Lewis County men. I remained as its commander until after the battle of Fredericksburg, when I was assigned to other duty. I was succeeded as Captain by George B. Winslow of Gouverneur. At the Battle of Gettysburg the battery belonged to the Third Corps, as it had belonged to that corps from its organization. In forming the line on the battlefield, Battery D was put into position not far from the center of Sickles's line and in what is known as the Wheatfield. The fighting in its immediate front was terribly severe and long continued, but in the end Sickles's line was forced back. The battery remained and fought until the infantry was driven beyond it, thus exposing it to the enemy's skirmishers and sharpshooters against whom it could not protect itself.

It remained in position and fighting until the enemy was close to it, a few yards only from it, when it was ordered to withdraw if it could do so. The battery drew out. The last section, two guns, to withdraw was commanded by Lieutenant L.J. Richardson, who attached prolonges and continued to fire the guns as he drew out. This was a feat performed but few times during the war and required soldierly qualities more often lacking than existing. It required an officer of steel nerves, the most perfect discipline of the men and obstinate bravery in both. Indeed, occasionally men under such trying and pressing conditions perform more heroic deeds than they conceive while performing them. No braver act than this was performed during the war. The other officers and men were not less brave, but the circumstances threw upon Richardson and his men the conditions which led to this specific act after long and desperate fighting. Winslow was wounded in the Wilderness, and Richardson commanded the battery during nearly all of Grant's Campaign in the east and until he was himself wounded south of Petersburg. Northern New York, or indeed any other section of the U.S., sent no better command into the war than Battery D.

In that engagement Sickles lost a leg. When put into the surgeon's hands, he refused to take chloroform. Lighting a cigar, he smoked while he watched the amputation of his leg halfway between the knee and hip.

However in connection with that part of the Battle of Gettysburg, a serious difficulty arose between Meade and Sickles as to whether Sickles obeyed orders in putting his corps into position in the general line of the army. Meade claimed that he did not obey orders and Sickles that he did. Meade also claimed that Sickles so exposed his line that he tempted Longstreet to attack, that Longstreet would not have done so but for that exposure. On this Meade was wrong. Longstreet states that Sickles's movements or position had nothing to do with his making the movement, as it had been decided upon the night before and he was already prepared to advance and should have attacked whether Sickles was there or not. It was a long controversy between Meade and Sickles and their friends, and the ill feelings gendered at the time are not yet wholly eradicated. It was an important part of the battle, and while Meade's army suffered severely, Lee's army suffered no less in his loss of men. At the close of the fight on that flank, Meade's entire line was reestablished and Lee was not again able to disturb it.[16]

 While the fighting was still in progress on Sickles's front, an effort was made by Ewell to force the pass at Rock Creek. Lee's orders were that both attacks by Longstreet and Ewell should be made at the same time. Longstreet waited some time to hear Ewell's guns, but not hearing them, attacked and his fight was far advanced before Ewell's attack. The Twelfth Corps was in the pass supported by the Pennsylvania Reserves. The Fifth Corps, which had been engaged with Longstreet, or a part of that corps, was returned to Slocum's aid.

 One of the greatest advantages of the Gettysburg Battlefield was its form as a crescent. Troops could be moved within the arc from one point in the line to another upon the shortest lines.

 Slocum's and Ewell's fight was on a comparatively narrow front and in the forests. The battle continued until night, when Ewell fell back. Slocum remained in the position he held from the first. It was not advisable or desirable for him to advance and establish a new and advanced line. He already had the best possible line. The extreme right of the First Corps had been weakened by drawing from it one or two brigades to fight Longstreet. Late in the afternoon the advanced breastworks these brigades had occupied were seized and held through the night by a detachment of Ewell's corps. They were driven out by a very severe fight and the works regained before sunrise the next morning.[17]

 While fighting by Longstreet against Sickles was in progress, I am not confident of the exact time, the enemy's skirmishers took possession of a brick house just outside of the cemetery gate and in the edge of the town. From its windows and loopholes they were actively picking off our officers and men, both infantry and artillery. They were wholly protected from the fire of our infantry as they were within the enemy's lines, and an advance to clear them from the house would have resulted in a battle and probably a failure to succeed. This was not desirable while the army was elsewhere engaged. We knew that the house was filled with enemy sharpshooters, but we did not know what else it contained or whether the family remained in it or not. The natural presumption was that the family had left when or before the enemy seized it for a fortress from which to fight. I do not remember that we considered that matter much, but after the sharpshooting became galling and the infantry could make no impression on it with their muskets, General Howard suggested that I clear the house with artillery. This I was very willing to do. I turned the fire of several guns on the house, and the shot and shell went into and through it as readily as rifle balls would go through cardboard. The artillery fire soon riddled the brick walls and cleared the house of the sharpshooters. Unfortunately, the family had remained in the house and a young lady was killed. The act of clearing the house from the sharpshooters, who were actively picking off our officers and men, was legitimate. The killing of the young lady was purely an accident of the battle. This incident has been frequently written about, and this house where she was killed is now one of the showplaces of the battlefield.[18]

All of the cemetery was occupied by the Eleventh Corps, and in it the batteries of the corps were in position. The gate of the cemetery was adjoining to the town. The main street of the town, which outside of the town became the Baltimore Road, passed the gate, and the houses were built up to the entrance. A few rods below the gate and in the town, the main street or Baltimore Road made a turn so that the houses completely screened the movements of the enemy within the town.

The picket line was too active for any scouts to get through and return with information as to what the enemy was doing. Howard did not know what force the enemy had in his immediate front occupying the town itself.

A little after sunset but while it was yet quite light, Early's division of Ewell's corps, having approached within a few rods of the cemetery gate, made a charge under cover of the houses on Howard's line at or near the gate. This force was within a few yards of the line before it was discovered. These troops made a sudden dash and assault to break Howard's line. In a minute they were among our men, and a hand-to-hand fight was in an exceedingly active progress. The front of the assault was narrow. Howard hurried other brigades to the assistance of the one assaulted, and Hancock sent one brigade from the Second Corps as a reinforcement.[19] After a severe struggle lasting about a half hour, the enemy was driven back and the line reestablished. Altogether, it was a violent fight by comparatively small fractions of the two armies, probably three or four thousand men on each side.

In connection with the fight of that evening, I wish to speak of the conduct of Battery I and of my own command in the Eleventh Corps.[20] The battery was commanded by Captain Wiedrich and was from Buffalo. Both officers and men were, in the main, Germans. The momentum of the enemy's charge carried them over the front line and into Wiedrich's and Rickett's regular batteries, which were just in rear of our line of battle. In a half minute when the enemy was making an effort to secure possession of the two batteries, the officers and men instantly began to fight to save their guns, using everything that they could lay their hand upon. They could no longer fire their guns as the enemy was in the battery. They seized the rammers, handspikes, fence rails, threw shot with their hands, and the officers used their sabres and pistols with remarkable activity and energy. Of course, all this lasted but two or three minutes, or even less, but it was sufficient to prevent the enemy from capturing the guns and hauling them through the gate and into the town.

As Early's command was driven back, Wiedrich at once took charge of his battery. He fought with the battery until Early was driven back and after that until the close of the war. In the fight First Lieutenant Salem of Wiedrich's battery was made a prisoner and taken into the edge of the town. In the stampede attendant upon Early's sudden repulse, he escaped and returned to his battery. However, while he was a prisoner, his sword was taken from him. His name, rank and battery was roughly sketched upon the sword with a knife. The rebel officer wearing the sword was captured early the next winter near the Rappahannock River in Virginia, and as Salem's name was on the sword, it was sent to the War Department and returned to Salem

Route of Gen. Harry T. Hay's Assault on East Cemetery Hill as Viewed from Wiedrich's Battery. *(Courtesy of the Gettysburg National Military Park.)*

who was then with me at Bridgeport, Alabama. In the hand-to-hand fight to save their guns, Rickett's regular battery had precisely the same experiences that Wiedrich's battery had. That battery fought no more nor less desperately than did Wiedrich's. Rickett's battery did not belong to my command, except temporarily.

With the close of the assault by Early on Cemetery Hill and his repulse, the fighting for the day closed. At dusk the line of Meade's army was everywhere perfect and as laid out, excepting one brigade of the First Corps where the advanced works were held by a division of Ewell's corps. Early the next morning that force was driven out and the line at that point reestablished as desired.[21]

There is one important point I should have mentioned earlier in speaking of this battle. This is in regard to the subdivisions of the army. The armies were about equal in numbers. Lee's army was subdivided into three corps, Meade's into seven. The divisions and brigades bore about the same relations in numbers to each other in the two armies, as the corps did. A division in Lee's army was much larger than a division in Meade's army, and a brigade in Lee's army was much larger than a brigade in Meade's army. As a rule, the corps, divisions and brigades of Lee's army were more than double in strength than the corps, divisions and brigades in Meade's army. In this particular, Lee's army had the best organization. With this knowledge of the organization of the two armies any study of the Battle of Gettysburg is simplified and can be better understood.

The Third Day

Excepting the recovery of the works on the right of the First Corps which was accomplished after a short fight, the morning of the Third Day of the battle and the third day of July was quiet. Nothing else occurred, except the sharp firing on the picket lines. That was nearly incessant along the entire front. Our line had not been changed in the night, except to strengthen it here and there at points where it was thought Lee would be most likely to attack. I do not know how much was known early in the day at army headquarters of Lee's movements. There was a general impression that he was massing his army in front of our left, that is he was moving the bulk of his army to his right in

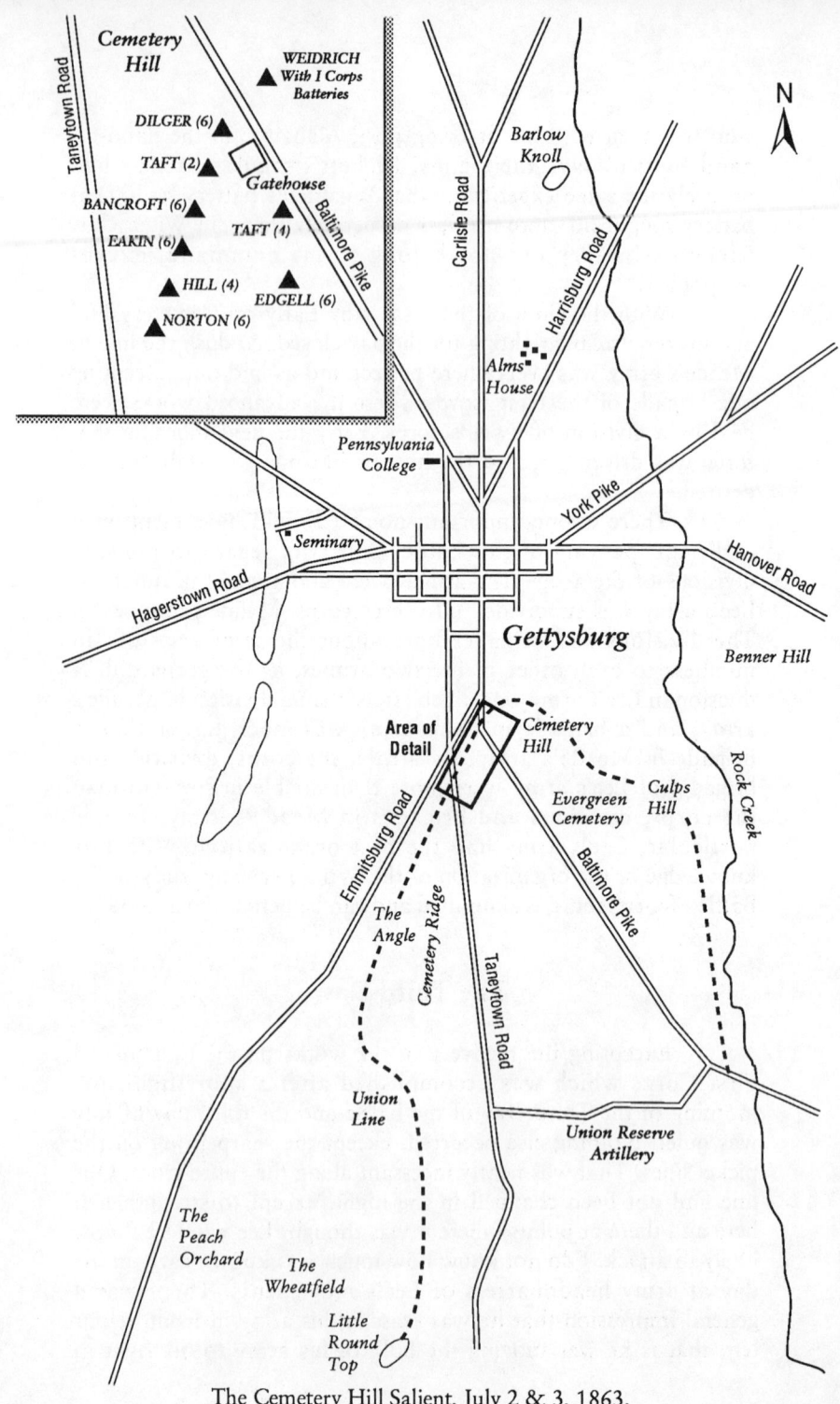

The Cemetery Hill Salient, July 2 & 3, 1863.
Inset: July 3, 1863; 3 p.m.

order to throw it against Meade's left. Before noon Meade was satisfied that the movement was being made. Our line was somewhat in the form of a horseshoe with one side longer than the other, the toe being towards the enemy. We were also in position, intrenched and on the defensive. We had the shorter line, but with Lee's army massed against one flank, this did not count for so much as if his army had been more extended. Still, in the main, these were all advantages. Lee had the advantage, on the other hand, of being free to mass his whole army, or as much of it as he chose, at one point and throw it against a weaker point of Meade's line. This he did.

During all the forenoon there was an ominous silence on the part of the enemy. It was reported to us from the Headquarters of the Army that the enemy could be seen moving along Seminary Ridge to a point opposite the left wing of the army. Batteries were being put into position all along Seminary Ridge to bear upon that wing of our army and commanding our entire front. The report was correct. Before the afternoon battle opened, with our glasses we could see Lee's batteries in position on Seminary Ridge, standing at regulation intervals covering a line of two miles. It was the longest and finest line of light batteries ever planted on a battlefield. We were fully aware that this line of batteries meant mischief to us and that immediately behind it was a corresponding body of infantry.

At precisely one o'clock in the afternoon we saw a puff of smoke from a gun fired from the hills upon our front and right, and about two and a half miles from us. Soon after, in less than a minute, the sharp whistle of a Whitworth bolt or shot, aimed at the crest of Cemetery Hill, passed a few feet over our heads.[22] The report from a Whitworth gun and the sound of the long steel bolt used for a solid shot, as it passes through the air, is readily recognized and distinguished from the reports of all other guns. By the time this Whitworth shot had passed us and gone to the rear of the army without doing harm, more than two hundred and fifty guns from Lee's line opened upon Meade's army.[23]

More than half of these were turned upon the small space of Cemetery Hill which I occupied with five batteries. They were turned upon the guns of my command. The crest of the hill was so limited that even the guns I had were placed at half regulation distance. I at once appreciated that the admirable position taken by Howard and especially the hill upon which he had placed his own command was fully recognized by the enemy as the point of greatest strength in the line. It was plain that Lee's primary object was to drive the artillery from that hill. He put his guns into position in the form of a crescent in such a manner that nearly all of them could bear upon Cemetery Hill. A little later, perhaps twenty minutes or a half hour, 36 guns were in position on our right so as to bring them directly on the flank of my line. They commanded my guns to absolute perfection.[24] With the opening of these last guns, the enemy's line of artillery was practically in a semi-circle around us. My batteries on the hill were then raked from every side, except the rear and the direct left. In addition to the military necessity of driving my guns from Cemetery Hill, we were upon the crest of an elevation and in plain view from every part of the enemy's line. We were an especially tempting object for every gun the enemy had, and more than half of them were devoted exclusively to us.

Instantly upon the enemy's guns opening fire, all the guns on Meade's front opened. Meade had as many guns in line as did Lee. The firing on both sides was exceedingly rapid, going up from two to four shots a minute from each gun on both sides. That is about as rapidly as the chief of the gun could take good aim.

Allowing that three shots a minute were fired by each gun, which was for a considerable time below the average, there were 1,500 shots a minute passing between the armies. If it should be thought that I overstate the number of shots which can be fired in a minute from a single muzzle loading gun, I will say that Battery D under pressure at the Battle of Chancellorsville fired nine shots a minute from every gun, or 54 shots a minute from six guns, and every one with good aim.[25] It does not take longer for a well-drilled battery to load and fire a cannon than for a sportsman to load and fire a fowling piece. The gun, under pressure, can be loaded and fired as fast as one man can bring ammunition from the ammunition chest which is generally about ten steps in rear of the gun.

At the moment the artillery fire opened, I had only the five batteries on the hill or 26 guns, but I acted upon General Hunt's instructions and called on the Artillery Reserve for about as many more, making all told on Cemetery Hill a little short of 50 guns. The space occupied was so small that the guns were placed at half distance and the batteries close together. I was determined to hold the hill no matter how severe the fire might be.

Taft's Section (2 guns) Near the Gatehouse, Facing West.

It is now conceded that never in any battle in the world was the fire of light artillery so heavy as that at Gettysburg. Every gun on the line in both armies was doing its best. The fire of both armies was excellent. Looking down our own line or along the enemy's line, there was not a half minute that one could not see the smoke from an exploded ammunition chest. A shell or solid shot striking a chest exploded it, and the white smoke from the powder shot up in a solid cloud which could be seen from every part of the army. These explosions were an indication of the accuracy of the fire and the damage being done by the fire of the opposing armies. More shot and shell killed men and horses than hit the small ammunition chests.

The sound was, of course, deafening, though little attention was paid to it. I am under the impression that the infantry paid far more attention to the sound of the guns than the artillery men did. I have often heard infantry officers speak of it, though I have but a faint recollection of it myself.

While the firing was at its height in our front and along the main line to our right, bringing a fire upon our line from a considerable angle, a group of guns (after the battle I learned to have been 36) opened square upon our right flank so as to rake my line its entire length. From the first shot they had our range and elevation exactly, and the havoc among my guns, men, horses and ammunition chests was fearful. Guns were hit and knocked off their carriages, ammunition chests were blown up and horses were going down by the half dozen. To meet this fire, I drew out from the line three batteries and swung them half around to face this new fire. The hill was so narrow that the guns were put as close together as they could be worked. These three batteries, in turn, got the range and elevation of the enemy's guns at the first fire, upon which the enemy lost our elevation at once and did very little more damage. After our guns began to play upon them, they fired very wildly. After the battle we visited the ground those batteries occupied and found they had been literally destroyed. Men, horses and the debris of the batteries showed that all those batteries were ruined.[26] I had only 14 guns to their 36. However, my command suffered a good deal from their fire but was not moved by it.

Our fire to the front and on the flank rapidly used up the ammunition, and I ordered the ammunition chests refilled from the army ordnance train while the fighting was in full progress. This was done by sending one, two or more caissons at a time to

Benner's Hill, East of the Baltimore Pike, from Taft's Position.

the train to have the chests filled.

As a rule, the fire of the enemy on all our front against Cemetery Hill was a little high. Their range or direction was perfect, but the elevation carried a very large proportion of their shells about twenty feet above our heads. The air just above us was full of shells and the fragments of shells. Indeed, if the enemy had been as successful in securing our elevation as they did the range there would not have been a live thing on the hill fifteen minutes after they opened fire. The batteries on our right flank did secure both range and elevation perfectly, but in a few minutes we so demoralized them that they lost the elevation but not the direction, and they too fired high. As it was, we suffered severely.

Under all human conditions where the surroundings are exceptionally pressing or serious, more or less ludicrous incidents will occur. This terrific artillery battle, which all knew was the immediate forerunner of victory or defeat, was no exception to that rule. I will mention a couple of them now and then go on with the narrative of the battle. During such time, the force of will which an officer must bring to bear upon himself in order not only to control his men but also to govern himself, is wonderful. He must by sheer force of will shut up every impulse of his nature, except that of controlling the officers and men subject to his command. He must discard all care of his personal safety and even his own life. The most difficult person to control is always himself.

I had before served under Generals Heintzelman, Hooker and Berry in battle, where I had an opportunity to learn what their peculiar characteristics were, and so far in that battle I had learned what Howard's peculiarities were.[27] The more desperate the conditions surrounding them, the more desperately cool and collected they bore themselves. Under the hottest fire and most trying circumstances, they were as polite and wore as pleasant a smile as if they were in the presence of ladies in a parlor. These officers and others like them, I had known and served with. The only prominent exception I had known to this rule was General Sumner whom I served under in the Battle of Savage Station. During a fight he appeared excitable to the last degree, but his command of troops on the field was perfect. With a smaller force than Magruder commanded in that battle, he whipped him in an hour.

While this fire on Cemetery Hill was at its very height,

General Meade rode into the batteries at great speed followed by two or three staff officers. As he came within hearing he shouted, "Where is Major Osborn?! Where is Major Osborn?!" As he came near me, I answered him. He then shouted, apparently greatly excited, "What are you drawing ammunition from the train for?" I said that some of the ammunition chests were giving out. He then said, "Don't you know that it is in violation of general orders and the army regulations to use up all your ammunition in a battle?" I replied that I had given that no thought and that General Hunt had directed me to draw what I might require from the ordnance train. He then said, "What do you expect to do here?" I replied that I was expected to hold the hill, and that I expected to do so, if the infantry would stand by me. To this he retorted, "You cannot hold your men here." I replied, "I will stay here, General, and so will my men."

He then rode off with as great a speed as he had come. He gave me no orders. Apparently he was greatly excited, but his command in the battle, from beginning to end, showed that his judgment was good and not influenced by his excitable nature. I have no doubt that Meade was as brave personally as any of the officers mentioned, but he was a passionate man and excitable, and in officer-like bearing upon a battlefield he bore no comparison to the others. This scene was far more ludicrous than serious. His reference to the army regulations and general orders under these circumstances was, to say the least, a little peculiar. Yet he gave me no orders, nor objected to my getting all the ammunition I might deem necessary.[28] At the time and after, I was under the impression that no one except those I mentioned were near, but years after, General Howard told me that he was standing near and heard all that passed between General Meade and myself.

Another incident occurs to me which at the time roused my temper considerably. In reply to my requisition from the Reserve Artillery for more batteries, an Ohio battery was sent to me, which I placed at the extreme left on my line and near a clump of forest trees, a little natural grove into which Cemetery Hill broke off abruptly. The battery had been under fire but a few minutes when information was brought to me that the men were throwing ammunition out of the chests into that bunch of timber. This was in order to get clear of it and then represent that it was expended and so retire from the field. I went to the battery, gave the captain some orders in emphatic English and then left him. A few minutes later several of the men called out, "Look, Major, see the cowards." I did look and saw that Ohio battery with all the men mounted on the ammunition chests going at full speed, the horses running down the Baltimore Pike, the drivers whipping their horses at every jump. I never saw that battery again, and as it did not belong to my command, I did not report it to its proper superiors. Doubtless, the captain reported to the commander of the Reserve Artillery that he was in the hottest of the fight and that he and all his men were heroes. At all events, the giant monument on Cemetery Hill stands today to the credit of that battery.[29]

Still another personal incident comes to me which impressed itself upon my mind because my personal vanity was a little set back. Captain Wadsworth, a son of General Wadsworth, was an aide on the staff of General Meade. I am under the impression that it was the same Wadsworth who of late years has figured largely in New York and national politics.[30] While the artillery fire was still at its highest, he came to me with some directions and to make some inquiries for headquarters. I was at the moment on a nice horse thoroughly accustomed to me. His horse was the same. We halted close together in the midst of the batteries, the horses headed in opposite directions and our faces near together. Neither horse flinched. The forelegs of each horse were in line with the hind legs of the other, and we stood broadside to the enemy's fire. While we were talking, a percussion shell struck the ground directly under the horses and exploded. The momentum of the shell carried the fragments along so that neither horse was struck nor did either horse move. When the shell exploded, I was in complete control of my nerves and did not move a muscle of my body or my face. Neither did Wadsworth, but I dropped my eyes to the ground where the shell exploded, and Wadsworth did not. I never quite forgave myself for looking down to the ground when that shell exploded under us. I do not believe that there was a man in the entire army, save Captain Wadsworth, who could have a ten pound shell explode under him without looking where it struck.

There were many other incidents of that afternoon which were photographed on my memory, but most of them were of a sad nature and involved suffering at an hour when no heartbeat of sympathy could be expressed. One in illustration of this order will be enough. One regular soldier who had served with me as an orderly for a considerable time was struck with a shell just as I arrived at his battery. His entire shoulder was torn out. He saw me as he fell, and with a word of affection and farewell, bled to death in a minute or two. This is sufficient of the many incidents of suffering which were every minute before our eyes on Cemetery Hill that afternoon.

General Hunt, Chief of Artillery of the Army, came upon the hill almost immediately after General Meade of whom I have spoken, but he dismounted to canvass the desperate state of affairs as the entire artillery of both armies was working up to its capacity, and there was no variation in the fire upon Cemetery Hill. As I was in charge of the artillery, Hunt was talking to me when Generals Howard and Schurz joined us. We were talking over the course of this fearful artillery duel and what might be Lee's plans, as the artillery fire was evidently intended to precede some more desperate movement of the infantry. It was conceded by all that the mass of Lee's army was concentrated behind Seminary Ridge and in front of Meade's left wing, between three-fourths of a mile and a mile from it. In our conversation we assumed these facts which afterward proved to be correct. We also believed that Lee's primary object was to drive the guns off of Cemetery Hill. This, Lee's Chief of Artillery has since written to me was a fact, as those guns more than any others in our army commanded the open plain over which his great charge was to be made.[31]

I said to these officers that I believed that if we should stop firing along our entire line suddenly and as though the artillery on Cemetery Hill was driven off the field, Lee would at once develop his plans—that if the General would give me permission, I would stop my batteries at once. Hunt said that he thought I was correct, and if Howard agreed to it, he would give the order. Howard thought the suggestion a good one and said that he would like to see the experiment tried. Hunt asked me if I could keep my men on the hill if I stopped their work, and expressed the belief that I could not hold them. I told him that I could do so and to give himself no uneasiness on that score. He then gave the order to stop firing and said that he would ride down the line and stop all the batteries.[32]

Then he left the hill, riding at great speed. All of this took but a few minutes; meanwhile there was no cessation of fire from any part of the field in either line, and shells were reaching the hill from 800 to 1,000 a minute. A few feet above our heads the air was nearly as full of shells and fragments of shells as it is of flakes in a snowstorm, and every second or two a shell struck among the batteries and men on the hill.

I went to my battery on the right, Wiedrich's, ordered him to cease firing and for every officer and man to lie flat upon the ground covering themselves as best they could by the unevenness of the ground, and to remain there until further orders.[33] From Wiedrich's battery I walked along the line and gave the same order to each battery, whether they belonged to my own command or were borrowed from the Artillery Reserve. This required but a very few minutes and every gun on the hill was silent, and the enemy's officers with their glasses could see none of our men on the hill. Hunt rode very rapidly along the line, and the batteries stopped one after another in quick succession. Meanwhile, the enemy's shells came in nearly as rapidly as before. In the same magazine article of which I have spoken, General Hunt claims to have originated the idea of stopping the fire of the artillery to tempt Lee to develop his plans. This moment was in fact the turning point in the battle in our favor, and Hunt made the most of it for himself. Fortunately, both Howard and Schurz were present at the time, and both have since publicly stated the facts to be as I have given them and would confirm them upon inquiry.

We had but a few minutes to wait after the artillery ceased firing for developments. I think it was not more than ten minutes before the enemy's line of battle showed itself coming over Seminary Ridge at the point where we supposed Lee's troops were massed. As the line of battle came into view, it appeared to be about three-fourths of a mile in length and was moving in perfect line. The moment that line appeared coming down the slope of Seminary Ridge, every battery on Meade's line opened on it. Lee believed that he had silenced all our batteries while, with the exception of one or two a couple of hundred yards beyond my left, none had been so seriously injured that they were not able to continue their fire. The enemy's artillery kept up their fire on our line, but none of our batteries paid any further attention to it. They devoted their attention exclusively to the advancing line of battle.

From the very first minute our guns created sad havoc in that line. Lee's first line of battle had advanced about two hundred yards, after it came within sight, when another line in every way similar followed. These two lines of battle, nearly a mile distant, were then the sole object of fire of all the guns which

Wartime Sketch by Edwin Forbes of the Artillery in the Cemetery.

could be made to bear upon them. The effects of this fire could very soon be seen. At first the distance was so great that only solid shot from the brass guns and percussion shells from the rifled guns could be effectively used. The artillerymen endeavored to roll the solid shot through the ranks and explode the percussion shells in front of the lines. This method was effective to a large degree, as we would see the ranks thinned at many points and here and there a wide gap made as from two to a dozen men were taken out by the men being shot down. All this made no impression on the movement of the double line of battle. The men moved as steadily as if on dress parade. The entire field was open, and the movement was in plain view on a nearly level plain.

As the lines advanced, both the rifled and smooth bore guns used time shells upon the advancing lines and the killing and wounding was proportionately more severe. When they had covered about one third of the distance from Seminary Ridge to our line, their ranks had been a good deal cut out. They halted and closed their ranks from the right and left on the center and dressed their lines, which were materially shortened. This was done under a fearful artillery fire which was cutting them down by the hundreds every minute. They then moved forward as before, but the nearer they approached the more severe was their loss from our guns and the more seriously were the lines thinned. Still there was no hesitation or irregularity in the movement. The steady and firm step of the veteran soldiers continued.

Again they made another third of the distance and were just within the long range of cannister by the artillery and musketry by the infantry when the lines again halted, closed up and dressed, still more depleted than before. The lines were then very materially shortened in comparison with what they were when they first came into view.

After leaving Seminary Ridge, the lines had moved at a quick step, not double quick. From this second halt, the charge proper was made at a double quick. From that point to about half the distance to Hancock's line, Lee's lines passed out of range of my guns as an elevation of ground cut them off from my sight. I then turned my guns to answer the enemy's artillery which had not ceased playing upon the hill.

The remainder of the charge upon Hancock's front was made upon the double quick over about an eighth of a mile and of course occupied but a very few minutes. In that few minutes they received the full shock of the musketry and cannister of our line in their front, as the guns on the flanks could no longer reach them. Still they were so rapidly cut down that the regular lines of battle could not be maintained. As they approached Hancock's line, as is always the case in such charges, they took advantage of the slight irregularities of the ground, formed themselves into wedge shape and made a dash in this form to break Hancock's line. They struck that line about a fourth of a mile to my left. They did break the line, and a little more than three thousand men passed through it and were immediately captured. The remainder were driven back or killed or wounded.

The break made in Hancock's line was open only long enough for the men captured to pass through and was then closed from the right and left while they were still passing. All not carried through by the momentum of the movement were turned back. Those who had gone through were immediately surrounded and captured. No other break was made in the line.

The repulse of this column of the 15,000 men commanded by Major General Pickett was completed. All that was left of Pickett's command hurried back to Seminary Ridge. No order was preserved in the retreat, as indeed none was possible. No two men remained together, but each one ran back as rapidly as he could to Lee's line. As the men were retreating in disorder over the plain, all of Meade's batteries again opened upon them and did them considerable damage, but of course not so much as when they were in a well organized line of battle. When the greater part of these men reached Lee's line, he ordered his artillery to cease firing. Ours immediately ceased, and the Battle of Gettysburg was finished. Meade had won the fight.

Pickett's charge at Gettysburg stands out by itself as the grandest charge made by any command during the war. I was in many great battles, but I never saw so superb and desperate a charge made and under conditions so favorable to view as that. The charges made by the several corps of Burnside's army at Fredericksburg were fully as desperate, but there was no chance of success. These charges were almost criminally foolish on Burnside's part. Lee's charge on Malvern Hill was worse and more foolish than was Burnside's at Fredericksburg. All these I saw from the best points of view, but there was no chance of success in either of them. Hazen's charge to carry Fort McAllister, near Savannah, was a splendid feat at arms. The fort was an immense fortification mounted with heavy and light guns and garrisoned with artillery and infantry troops. The earth walls were 20 feet high and the whole work surrounded by abatis and planted with torpedoes, and yet he carried it with an infantry charge.

Sherman's battle at Kennesaw Mountain was, in fact, a grand charge upon the enemy's works and up the steep side of a rugged mountain. I did not witness that. This, like Pickett's charge, had the chance of success in it and was worth the attempt. Sheridan's charge up the flank of Missionary Ridge, which I saw, was eminently successful. He lost heavily, but broke Bragg's line and cut his army in two. Hooker's charge up Lookout Mountain, which I also saw, was successful and a grand success of arms. At Dalton, in the same battle, he made a charge and while he won on the ground, his force was so crippled that he could not take advantage of his success. At that, I was not present. Taking it all in all, Pickett's charge, although a failure, was the grandest of them all. Although they were our enemies at the time, those men were Americans, of our own blood and our own kindred. It was the American spirit which carried them to the front and held them there to be slaughtered. Phenomenal bravery is admired by everyone, and that Pickett's men possessed.

The remainder of the afternoon and evening, Lee held his army in position to see if Meade would make a counter charge. This was not made, and in the night Lee commenced his retrograde movement towards the Potomac River and Virginia. Meade's army had suffered severely, and the next day after the battle, the Fourth of July, he rested it and hastened to put it into condition to follow Lee south. He rested two days before commencing the pursuit of Lee. So great a delay was unfortunate, if not an error. No matter how greatly we were worn, Lee's army was still more worn and exhausted, and for that reason we should have had an advantage in a pursuit. The day following the battle was raining. It was used to care for the wounded and to bury the dead, as we prepared to move again.

I lost in the battle about 100 horses. The government had no spare horses with the army or anywhere immediately available. Unless these horses were replaced, I should be compelled to dismount one battery, take its horses for the others and leave it. This was not advisable. I therefore asked General Howard for an order to send men into the country and gather up the horses required from the citizens, in other words, press them into service. This order he gave, and I sent out the quartermaster sergeants of all the batteries with instructions to take from the citizens the horses that each battery required and give memoranda receipts for them. The orders were carried out to the letter and much to the consternation of the farmers. The receipts were given, and the government soon after paid $125 for each horse without inquiring as to its market value. It was a good sale for some, a bad one for others.

After waiting two days, Meade undertook the pursuit of Lee. He overtook his rear guard at Hagerstown, while the body of his army was entrenched on the bank of the Potomac at Williamsport. The Army of the Potomac was brought up in front of Lee's Army, and Meade occupied a day in preparing to attack. In the night Lee crossed the Potomac into Virginia and for the time being was out of reach of the Army of the Potomac.

Editor's note: *Osborn's description of the events of July 3rd on Cemetery Hill and his graphic account of the Pickett-Pettigrew assault center on events that he personally witnessed and vividly recalled.*

Unlike the First Day, his guns on the Second and Third Days fired from relatively stationary positions within or near the cemetery, making it less difficult to locate their positions. Some of the batteries present on the Second Day had been removed on the third. Hall's First Corps, Maine Battery was engaged only on the second, and Wheeler's battery of Osborn's brigade retired to the reserve after the Second Day. It was rushed to the Angle near Rorty's battery at the climax of Pickett's assault.

There was some movement among the five reserve batteries assigned to Osborn. On the Third Day Edgell's First New Hampshire Battery was initially placed in a cornfield in the rear of the cemetery to face east. On the afternoon of the third he took over Norton's position on the western edge of the hill, as Norton retired to the reserve. Near the end of the struggle, McCartney's Sixth Corps, First Massachusetts Battery briefly occupied Edgell's position, as the latter retired.

Of the five batteries in Osborn's brigade only Dilger and Bancroft occupied their original positions during Longstreet's assault on the third. Of the reserve, four of Taft's 20-pounders faced east on the Baltimore Pike and two, placed between Dilger and Bancroft, fired to the west. At 3 p.m., three of Taft's guns on

Evergreen Cemetery Gatehouse, 1863.
(Courtesy of the Gettysburg National Military Park.)

the Pike relieved the section in the cemetery (one had "burst at the muzzle"). Eakin's Battery H, First U.S. and Hill's Battery C, First West Virginia from the reserve maintained their positions, facing west on both days.

On the Second and Third Days one more of the reserve batteries, as well as Taft's guns on the Baltimore Pike, were used by Osborn to counter Confederate artillery fire from the east, and on those occasions were moved to the right and rear of Taft's four guns to face east.

The following estimate of the number of guns Osborn had in the cemetery on the afternoon of the third during the Confederate infantry assault is made from the battle reports of Hunt, Osborn and the battery commanders:

12-pounders (Dilger, Bancroft & Eakin, 6 each) 18
20-pounders (Taft)...3
10-pounders (Hill) 4
3-inch rifles (Norton or Edgell).....................................6
                                                          Total 31

Only three of Taft's six guns fired to the west. Although Edgell and Norton each had six guns, they were engaged at different times. Only six of Wainwright's guns were able to fire from East Cemetery Hill, four from Wiedrich's battery and two from Rickett's.

Notes

[1] Union returns of June 30 for infantry and artillery units show 100,000 men present for duty. Confederate returns of May 31 show an aggregate of 60,000 men. It is probably accurate to deduct 10% of these numbers for those men not present for combat on July 1, the sick, stragglers and those men absent without leave.

[2] Dilger arrived first, followed half an hour later by Wheeler.

[3] Howard was probably on the Carlisle Road. Osborn may have confused Pennsylvania College with the Lutheran Seminary. He was misinformed about the early withdrawal of the First Corps. It and the Eleventh Corps withdrew around 4 o'clock. Unfamiliar with the terrain held by the First Corps, he confuses Seminary and McPherson Ridges.

[4] Heckman should read Dilger. Heckman's battery became actively engaged much later at the time of the Eleventh Corps' withdrawal from its position northeast of town. The battery's monument is located at the intersection of the Carlisle and Harrisburg (Heidlersburg) Roads.

[5] Wilkeson's battery was attached to Barlow's division, and the "bluff" referred to has become known as Barlow's Knoll.

[6] Osborn initially left Heckman, not Dilger, in reserve on Cemetery Hill along with Wiedrich. He later moved Heckman's battery to a position just north of the town. Apparently as he returned to the Eleventh Corps position, he found Wheeler and Dilger, not Heckman, returning to town.

[7] Osborn probably accompanied Wheeler and Heckman during their difficult escape through Gettysburg. Dilger took a different, more circuitous route to Cemetery Hill in order to escape the congestion caused by the retreat of the First and Eleventh Corps.

[8] Lt. Col. George Arrowsmith was a member of the 157th NY Volunteer Infantry, and had graduated from Madison University in 1859.

[9] In his journal, Wainwright wrote that Howard placed him in command of all the artillery on Cemetery Hill, even though the official reports of Howard, Hancock and Wainwright, himself, make no mention of this arrangement. Osborn claimed that Howard had placed him in command of the batteries west of the Baltimore Pike in the cemetery.

[10] Osborn seems to be overly dramatic about Howard's determination "to fight to the end" and overestimates the strength of Confederate forces available for an early attack. Neither Johnson's division of Ewell's corps nor Anderson's division of A.P. Hill's corps were present and in position to attack.

[11] Reynolds fought to hold McPherson's Ridge, not to gain possession of Seminary Ridge.

[12] Osborn is anxious to give Howard credit for the selection of Cemetery Hill as a defensive position and repeats Howard's claim for that credit.

[13] He seems to downplay the arrival of Hancock on Cemetery Hill, an event generally heralded by the other Union officers and men. Hancock relieved Howard, his senior in rank, by Meade's order. Slocum upon his arrival took command. Osborn admired Howard and may have resented Hancock's arrival and Howard's demotion.

[14] During the night of July 1, Geary's Second Division of the Twelfth Corps occupied the extreme left of the Union line at Little Round Top and Ruger's First Division was located south of Rock Creek, leaving a

gap between it and the right of Wadsworth's First Corps division on Culp's Hill. Osborn's early morning observation of this unprotected Union right flank was correct. The "gorge" along Rock Creek was open to a Confederate advance. Kathleen Georg Harrison, Gettysburg National Military Park Historian estimates that Hunt later placed 47 First, Eleventh and Twelfth Corps guns along the Baltimore Pike to cover the temporary gap on Culp's Hill, following Slocum's request for artillery support.

15 Osborn apparently refers to Johnson's attack on Culp's Hill on the evening of July 2, a move made in conjunction with Early's assault against East Cemetery Hill.

16 Like many other Civil War combatants, Osborn cannot resist the urge to express an opinion, to go on record in the Meade-Sickles controversy.

17 Longstreet's attack had ceased before Ewell launched his attack on East Cemetery and Culp's Hills, which allowed Hancock to dispatch Carroll's brigade of the Second Corps to the relief of the Union forces on East Cemetery Hill. The long and bitter struggle to recapture the entrenchments on Culp's Hill occupied by Johnson's division on the night of July 2 lasted until 11 a.m. on July 3. The works had been abandoned by Ruger and two brigades of Geary's Twelfth Corps divisions when Meade ordered them to support the left of the Union line, under assault by Longstreet.

18 The target of Osborn's guns was not the house in which Jennie Wade was killed. He mistakenly took responsibility for Gettysburg's only civilian casualty.

19 The 58th and 119th NY Regiments of Krzyzanowski's Eleventh Corps brigade assisted in the recapture of Wiedrich's battery.

20 Battery I served under Wainwright on July 2 and 3. While critical of the battery commander, Wainwright praised the fighting qualities of the gun crews.

21 The entrenchments occupied by Ewell's men belonged to the Twelfth Corps.

22 The Whitworths were located on Oak Hill and opened fire within seconds after the Washington artillery's signal guns on Seminary Ridge.

23 Alexander counted 172 Confederate artillery pieces participating in the cannonade. Kathleen Georg Harrison, Gettysburg National Military Park Historian, estimates that 124 Union guns responded at one time or another to the Confederate bombardment.

[24] Alexander identified these guns as Milledge's battery of Nelson's battalion of Ewell's Reserve Artillery, whose three rifled guns fired 48 rounds, the only rounds fired by Nelson's 13 guns.

[25] Osborn seems to exaggerate.

[26] The "debris" discovered by Osborn after the battle belonged to Latimer's battery on Benner's Hill on the Second Day. Milledge's Georgia battery of 20-pounder Parrotts were fired on the Third Day from a position across from and north of the Hanover Road from Latimer at a range of 2500 yards.

[27] Osborn had served under Heintzelman during the 1862 Peninsula Campaign and with Hooker and Berry at Chancellorsville.

[28] This account of the conversation is more detailed and critical of the Commanding General than the earlier account in the *Philadelphia Weekly Times*. See Appendix B.

[29] See Appendix C.

30. Probably Capt. Craig Wadsworth, son of Gen. James S. Wadsworth, who served with distinction as a First Corps staff officer. He died in 1872 at the age of 31. His brother, James Wolcott Wadsworth, was a successful politician.

[31] Col. E.P. Alexander, who acted as the Confederate First Corps Artillery Chief on July 3.

[32] The decision to silence the Union artillery as a ploy to lure out the Confederate infantry may well have been an idea shared by Hunt, Meade and Osborn. Hunt gave the order to the other Union batteries along the line directly after leaving Cemetery Hill.

[33] Osborn considered Wiedrich to have been under his direct command. The contour of Cemetery Hill prevented the First Corps batteries east of the Baltimore Pike from firing at the advancing Confederate infantry.

Appendix A

Report of Maj. Thomas W. Osborn,
First New York Light Artillery,
commanding Artillery Brigade,
Eleventh Army Corps.
(From the Official Records, Pp.747-751)

> Headquarters Artillery, Eleventh Corps,
> July 29, 1863.

Sir: I have the honor to report, concerning the part borne by this command in the battle of Gettysburg on the 1st, 2d, and 3d instant, that on the morning of the 1st instant I moved from Emmitsburg toward Gettysburg with the artillery of the corps, consisting of five batteries, and marched in the following order: Captain Dilger in advance with the Third Division, Lieutenant Wheeler with the First Division and in the center, the three remaining batteries following closely in rear of the center division.

I herewith enumerate the batteries of the command: Battery G, Fourth U.S. Artillery, commanded by Lieut. B. Wilkeson, six light 12-pounders; Battery I, First Ohio Artillery, commanded by Capt. H. Dilger, six light 12-pounders; Battery K, First Ohio Artillery, commanded by Capt. L. Heckman, four light 12-pounders; Battery I, First New York Artillery, commanded by Capt. M. Wiedrich, six 3-inch, and Thirteenth New York Independent Battery, commanded by First Lieut. W. Wheeler, four 3-inch guns. Total, 26 guns.

After moving 5 or 6 miles, I received notice from Major-General Howard that the First Corps was already engaged with the enemy at Gettysburg, and that I should move the artillery to the front as rapidly as possible.

A little after 10 a.m. the first battery (Dilger's) reached the town, and was ordered by General Schurz to the front of and 300 yards beyond the town, where he took position, and at once became engaged with a rebel battery about 1,000 yards in its front. This battery was soon supported by another, when Captain Dilger was compelled to stand the fire from both until the arrival of Wheeler's battery half an hour later, when I ordered Lieutenant Wheeler to report to Captain Dilger. The result of this artillery duel was one piece of Wheeler's battery dismounted and five pieces of the enemy's, which they left upon the ground; besides, they lost comparatively heavier than we in horses and materiel.

During the short struggle both batteries changed position several times, and did so with excellent results and in the best possible manner, Captain Dilger using much judgment in the selection of his several positions. They did not leave their immediate locality until the corps was ordered by the commanding general to fall back to Cemetery Hill.

About 11 a.m. Lieutenant Wilkeson reached the field, and was ordered to report to General Barlow, commanding the First Division, which was engaged about three-fourths of a mile from the town and on the left of the York pike. The battery was assigned position by General Barlow, and when I reached the ground I found it unfortunately near the enemy's line of infantry, with which they were engaged, as well as two of his batteries, the concentrated fire of which no battery could withstand. Almost at the first fire, Lieutenant Wilkeson was mortally wounded, and carried from the field by 4 of his men. The command of the battery now devolved upon Lieutenant Bancroft. By changing position several times, the battery maintained its relative position until the division fell back to the town, when it retired to Cemetery Hill. During this engagement the battery was separated into sections or half batteries, and its struggle to maintain itself was very severe and persistent.

Captain Heckman was not ordered in until the corps had begun to fall back. He was then put into position, with a view of holding the enemy in check until the corps had time to retire through the town to the hill beyond, and though he worked his battery to the best of his ability, the enemy crowded upon it, and was within his battery before he attempted to retire. He was compelled to leave one gun in the hands of the enemy. I think no censure can be attached to this battery for the loss of the gun. The battery was so severely disabled otherwise that I was compelled to send it to the rear, thus losing the benefit of it during the fight of the second and third days.

Captain Wiedrich was assigned, on his arrival upon the field, to a position on the hill immediately in front of the cemetery entrance and overlooking the town. He was engaged several times during the day with the enemy's artillery at long range. He maintained the same position during the three days' fighting, but on this p.m. Colonel Wainwright, chief of artillery First Corps, took command of his battery, with the artillery on that side of the Baltimore pike. The artillery of the corps ceased firing for the day, when the corps fell back to Cemetery Hill.

I would remark here that during the p.m. of the 1st and the a.m. of the 2d, I furnished Colonel Wainwright, chief of artillery First Corps, with ammunition from the Eleventh Corps train, the train of the First Corps not being within reach. This of necessity caused considerable annoyance later in the engagement, on account of the difficulty in procuring a supply of ammunition sufficient to cover the great expenditure we were compelled to make through the engagement.

On the morning of the 2d, I applied to General Hunt, chief of artillery Army of the Potomac, for a greater amount of artillery than we then had, as our position was finely adapted to its use, and I did not consider that we had sufficient to assist our small infantry force in holding the position if the enemy should attack us in heavy force. The following batteries were ordered to report to me: Battery H, First U.S. Artillery, Lieutenant Eakin, six light 12-pounders; Fifth New York Independent Battery, Captain Taft, six 20-pounder Parrotts; Battery C, First West Virginia Artillery, Captain Hill, four 10-pounder Parrotts; Battery H, First Ohio Artillery, Captain Huntington, six 3-inch rifles; Second Maine Battery, Captain Hall, four 3-inch rifles; First New Hampshire Battery, Captain [Edgell] six 3-inch rifles. Total, 32.

Heckman's battery having been sent to the rear and one gun of Wheeler's battery dismounted, gave us on the morning of the 2d a total of fifty-two guns.

In the morning, before General Slocum had occupied his position, and while he was doing so, I placed three batteries on the right of the Baltimore road, commanding the ravine between the two prominent hills on our right; yet, as General Slocum withstood every assault on his lines without assistance, later in the day I withdrew these batteries to the hill. As soon as the enemy developed the position he would probably occupy with his batteries, I placed mine in position commanding them. By the assignment on the hill, Dilger had the right, resting next the Baltimore road and parallel with the Emmitsburg road; on his left, and in order, were Bancroft, Eakin, Wheeler, Hill, and Hall, commanding the enemy's batteries to the right of the town; and across the Baltimore road I placed Taft in rear of and perpendicular to Bancroft; also Huntington in rear of and perpendicular to Wheeler, but farther in the rear of Wheeler than Taft was of Bancroft, so that Taft's battery would not obstruct his line of fire.

By this assignment of artillery, I commanded with a reputable number of guns every point on which the enemy could place artillery commanding Cemetery Hill. I also occupied every point of the hill available for artillery, and during the engagement every gun, at different times, was used with good effect, and the fire of no one gun interfered with the fire of another. A sharp curve in the side of the hill also afforded good and convenient protection for the caissons. Most of the day the firing of the enemy's artillery was irregular, they scarcely opening more than one battery at a time, and when they did so we readily silenced them.

On our entire front the enemy held a fine crest for the protection of artillery, at a distance of 1,000 to 1,400 yards from us; but at the time the heavy attack was made on the extreme left of our line, the firing was very severe, and especially upon the hill. They engaged the greater portion of our whole line, and from both the right and left of the town much of the fire was concentrated on our position, but we soon gained a decided advantage over them, and long before the infantry struggle on the left was decided, we had silenced most of their guns.

In this artillery fire, Lieutenant Eakin was wounded in the hip, and carried from the field.

Between 7 and 8 o'clock in the evening, a rebel brigade charged from the town upon the hill and upon Captain Wiedrich's battery. The charge was very impetuous, and the infantry at first gave way, and the battery was held for a moment by the enemy, when the cannoneers rallied with the infantry, and, seizing upon any weapons they could reach, threw themselves upon the enemy, and assisted to drive them back. All was done that could be, both before and after the repulse of the enemy, by the use of canister upon their ranks.

Colonel Wainwright speaks in highly complimentary terms of both officers and men for their gallant conduct on this occasion. Although the command was much exhausted by the two days' work, most of the night was passed in replenishing the batteries with ammunition and making repairs.

On the morning of the 3d, we were in position the same as on the 2d, but little was done during the a.m. by our corps. Occasionally a rebel battery would open upon the cemetery, evidently with a view to obtain the exact elevation and time to make their fire effective in the p.m.'s work on our position. At each attempt we silenced them, with but little loss to ourselves.

About 2 p.m. they opened along our whole front with an unbroken line of artillery, and also heavily on our right flank, apparently using every description of missiles and field artillery. The crest which the enemy occupied varied from 1,000 to 1,900 yards distance, and afforded an excellent protection. I judge that the guns of not less than one-half mile of this front were concentrated on our position, besides several batteries on our right, which enfiladed our position, excepting Captains Taft's and Huntington's batteries.

Our artillery endured this fire with surprising coolness and determination. No battery even showed a disposition to retire, and several times during the cannonading we silenced several of their batteries, but at a moment's cessation on our part they would reopen upon us. The fire was extremely galling, and by comparing the rapidity with which the shells fell among and passed by our guns with the rapidity with which our guns replied, the number of guns playing on the hill was very much greater than the number in position there; probably double.

Our guns were worked with great coolness, energy, and judgment, but as no satisfactory results were obtained, I ordered all our guns to cease firing, and the men to lie down to await developments. At the same time the artillery of our entire front ceased firing, and a few moments later the infantry of the enemy broke over the crest from where the artillery had been playing, and made their grand charge across the plain upon our lines. The left of the charging column rested on a line perpendicular to our front, then stretching away to the right beyond our view, thus offering an excellent front for our artillery fire. We used, according to distance, all descriptions of projectiles. The whole force of our artillery was brought to bear upon this column, and the havoc produced upon their ranks was truly surprising.

The enemy's advance was most splendid, and for a considerable distance the only hindrance offered it was by the artillery, which broke their lines fearfully, as every moment showed that their advance under this concentrated artillery fire was most difficult; and though they made desperate efforts to advance in good order, were unable to do so, and I am convinced that the fire from the hill was one of the main auxiliaries in breaking the force of this grand charge. But while the enemy was advancing, and after having been repulsed, I insisted that the artillery fire should be turned intensely upon the infantry, and no notice whatever was to be taken of their artillery.

I am not able to speak of any one or more batteries as deserving especial notice over another. Every battery did its whole duty; the officers proved themselves brave and efficient, and the men on the battle-field were most willing, brave, and gallant; in fact, the only fault I could mention was too great willingness to use ammunition at small squads of men and on unimportant objects, yet this was not carried to excess.

The artillery of the reserve proved all that could be expected or even asked of it; without their assistance I do not conceive how I could have maintained the position we held. I feel most thankful for their assistance, and the very willing and cordial manner in which it was rendered.

I would also speak of Lieut. George W. Freeman, acting assistant adjutant-general of the command, for the great assistance he was to me and to the whole command during the engagement.

I am unable to give any definite estimate of the amount of ammunition expended during the engagement. After we had exhausted the supply with the batteries, I replenished from our train. Colonel Wainwright, on the p.m. of the 1st, also replenished from our train, and, after this source was exhausted, I drew from the reserve train of the army.

The casualties of this command are as follows.[See below.]

Our loss in pieces and horses is as follows:

Horses Killed

Battery G, Fourth U.S. Artillery. 31
Battery I, First Ohio Artillery (one piece disabled) 28
Battery K, First Ohio Artillery (one piece lost) 9
Battery I, First New York Artillery (one piece dismounted) 18
Thirteenth New York Independent Battery
(one piece dismounted). 12

         Total.........................98

I am, respectfully, your obedient servant,
       T. W. OSBORN,
Major, Commanding Artillery, Eleventh Corps.
      General Henry J. Hunt,
Chief of Artillery, Army of the Potomac.

Editor's note: *The casualties appeared in a revised statement on p.183 of the OR, and are herewith presented.*

	Killed Off	Killed EM	Wounded Off	Wounded EM	Captured or Missing Off	Captured or Missing EM	Total
1st NY Lt, Battery I		3	2	8			13
NY Light, 13th Battery				8		3	11
1st Ohio Lt, Battery I.				13			13
1st Ohio Lt, Battery K.		2	1	10		2	15
4th US, Battery G	1	1	—	11		4	17
Total Artillery Brigade	1	6	3	50		9	69

Appendix B

Philadelphia Weekly Times Article

Editor's Note: Osborn's *Philadelphia Weekly Times* article, written nearly sixteen years after the battle of Gettysburg, was apparently widely read by his contemporaries. E. Porter Alexander, who directed the massive Confederate artillery fire on the afternoon of July 3, 1863, found the account noteworthy enough to comment on it in both his memoirs, *Military Memoirs of a Confederate* and *Fighting for the Confederacy*. In the latter account he indicated his intent to include Osborn's article as an appendix.

Osborn seemed to confirm Alexander's post-war critique that the Southern high command failed to exploit fully the weakness in the most vulnerable part of the Union position, that salient formed as the line curved fishhook-like around Cemetery Hill. Its western face was open to an infantry attack from the Bliss farm lane, the position occupied by Rode's division after the evening of July 2nd. The First and Eleventh Corps guns on Cemetery Hill, according to Alexander, were vulnerable to an enfilade fire from Ewell's guns east of the salient. Firing from Benner's Hill in the afternoon of the 2nd, the fire of Latimer's battery or Ewell's corps proved ineffective. His outmanned guns were overwhelmed by Union guns of the First, Eleventh, and Twelfth Corps firing from Cemetery and Culp's Hills. However, on the following afternoon the short-lived, but effective burst of fire from one of Ewell's reserve batteries had a devastating impact on Cemetery Hill before being silenced by Taft's 20-pounders. Osborn described both artillery duels.

Weekly Times,
Philadelphia,
Saturday May 31, 1879,
Vol. III. No. 14

Annals of the War/Chapters of Unwritten History/ The Artillery at Gettysburg/An Account of the Operations at Cemetery Hill/ General Howard's Position/The Work of the Batteries Described by an Artillery Chief.

By Col. Thomas W. Osborn, U.S. Vols.
Late United States Senator from Florida

I intend to deal with but little in this article except the part borne by the artillery in position on Cemetery Hill, west of the Baltimore pike, at the battle of Gettysburg. I shall not attempt to designate the position of other troops or speak of what they did, excepting as may be necessary in writing of the artillery which was under my command. Nor do I, in any way, intend to review the strategy of the campaign or the grand tactics of the battle. The right grand division of the army, commanded by General Reynolds, comprising the First and Eleventh corps, were, on the morning of July 1, moving to Gettysburg by the way of the Emmitsburg road. General Reynolds, with the First corps, was in advance. As General Buford, with a cavalry division, had entered Gettysburg the evening before and found himself in the neighborhood of the enemy, the right grand division was being hurried on to Gettysburg as rapidly as possible. The First corps had camped the night previous six miles from Gettysburg and the Eleventh corps at Emmitsburg, eleven miles from the town. At 10 A.M. General Howard received notice from General Reynolds that he had engaged the enemy and was met by largely superior numbers, and urged General Howard to hurry his corps forward as rapidly as possible. The head of the Eleventh corps had at this time just come in sight of Gettysburg. I was with General Howard when he received this notice from General Reynolds, but the batteries were back marching with the column. One battery was marching with General Schurz's division and one with General Steinwehr's division. The remaining three were together between the two rear divisions. General Howard, directing me to bring the batteries forward as rapidly as possible, rode to the front. The next I saw him was after we had become engaged with the enemy. He was then near the Seminary road, north of the town.

The Artillery Brigade

The artillery of each corps of the army had previously been organized into a brigade and placed under the command of the chief of artillery of the corps, who reported to and was subject to the immediate command of the corps commander. I was at this time chief of artillery of the Eleventh corps. I noticed that General Howard, in a review of the battle, speaking of the artillery in the battle of the 1st of July, speaks of the reserve artillery of the corps under my command and that with General Schurz and General Steinwehr's divisions as belonging to those divisions. This is merely technical. In our march, one battery each had been ordered to march with these two divisions and the remaining three batteries together. In going into this action these batteries remained temporarily with the divisions. Subsequently, when the divisions had retired to Cemetery Hill the batteries were again brought together under my immediate command. General Howard does not afterward speak of them as assigned or reserve batteries. Indeed, from the moment any of the troops became engaged I took command of them all. At 11:30 A.M. General Howard received notice of General Reynolds' death, and being next in rank, took command of the grand division and General Schurz took command of the Eleventh corps. I reached Gettysburg in an hour, after receiving General Howard's order, with the batteries, and as the infantry moved through the town to the front I sent with them four batteries—Wheeler and Heckman to the left on the Seminary road, and Dilger and Wilkeson to the right, with General Barlow's division.[1] The remaining battery, Captain Wiedrich, I left at Cemetery Hill with General Steinwehr. This distribution of the batteries was under general instructions from General Howard. In person I first went with Wheeler and Heckman and placed those batteries about three-fourths of a mile from the town, on the left of the Seminary road. After they were well at work, I went over to Dilger's and Wilkeson's batteries, with General Barlow's division on the extreme right of Cemetery Ridge. On my way to General Barlow's division I met First Lieutenant Wilkeson, commanding Battery G, Fourth United States Artillery, being brought to the rear, having one leg cut off at the knee with a solid shot. He died a few hours later.

The fighting, which had been in progress by the First corps since morning, continued after I reached the field with great severity till we finally withdrew to Cemetery Hill between 4 and 5 o'clock in the afternoon. At every point where I saw the enemy's lines they extended beyond the flanks of our line. The artillery was exceedingly active, and each battery changed position repeatedly to meet the movements of the enemy's infantry and artillery. General Howard was making an effort to hold back the enemy until assistance could reach us from the other corps to which he had sent for relief. The enemy were overwhelming us with numbers, and the best that could be done was to make a stubborn resistance against the superior force moving against us. In this resistance the four batteries of the Eleventh corps at the front did all that lay in their power. General Howard, having concluded he could not hold the ground west of the town, and having done all that lay in his power with the small number of troops under his command, determined a little after 4 o'clock in the afternoon to withdraw through Gettysburg to Cemetery Hill. He had lost many men and had held the enemy in check until well along in the day. His troops could stand the pounding no longer and he determined to place them in a defensive position on Cemetery Hill. This place he had selected as a position on which to retire before he had passed through Gettysburg on the way to the front. As he states, in his article in the *Atlantic Monthly*, of July, 1870, he selected it as "the best position in which to locate my command." This selection was made without consulting other officers excepting his assistant adjutant general and without knowing that other officers had selected or thought of this immediate site for a battle-field.

General Howard's Movement

Having determined to withdraw his two corps to the hill, he first withdrew the First corps which had been engaged some hours the longest and had suffered the most severely—from the front of the enemy under cover of the Eleventh corps. Consequently the work I had to perform in this movement was to aid the infantry of the Eleventh corps to check the advance of the enemy while the First corps was being withdrawn to the rear. We were in no sense, during the withdrawal of the corps, taking the offensive, but having taken position on the north and west of the city were holding the ground until our front was cleared of the troops of the First corps, and the enemy were compelled to stop their advance in our front, and then hold our ground until the First corps and the detachments of the Eleventh corps, which had not passed through the city, were finally in position on Cemetery Hill. In accomplishing this the fighting by the infantry and artillery of the Eleventh corps was heavy, and both infantry and artillery suffered severely. After the First corps was in position on the hill the Eleventh corps was withdrawn through the city to the hill—the enemy followed us closely, killing and wounding many men in the streets.[2] I had one caisson wheel broken by a shot from the enemy's guns while we were passing through, and several horses were struck by musket balls while we were in the streets. About 5 o'clock in the afternoon the two corps were in position on the hill and the enemy ceased to attack that evening. During all the time we were retiring to the hill and until we were firmly upon it the enemy followed us closely and pressed us hard.

I will say a few words here as to who selected Cemetery Hill and Ridge as the battle-field, and how I understood the matter at the time. A distinction should be made, I think, between Cemetery Hill and Cemetery Ridge—the hill comprising only that ground on which the cemetery is, west of the Baltimore pike, and the remainder of the same elevation east of the Baltimore pike; the ridge, the flank extensions of the hill proper and extending to Round Top on the south and Culp's Hill on the east. These flank extensions are composed of a ridge elevated above the plain, but considerably lower than the hill proper. Some writers speak of the hill and ridge, others of the hill only, but meaning both the hill and ridge. I am not familiar with the local designations. Much has been said on this subject, and I have noticed the credit of the selection of this ridge, upon which the battle was fought, has been claimed by many for one general or another. The movement of the army to Gettysburg was, of course, made by General Meade, and the result being the battle of Gettysburg, must be credited to him. But as to who selected the identical ground between the mountains and which line gave us so great an advantage, appears to have been a matter of controversy. General Howard says that while looking for a position in which to put his troops, he ascended Cemetery Ridge, and seeing the advantages of the ridge for a defensive line, said to Colonel Meizenburg:[3] "This seems to be a good position." The colonel replied that "It is the only position." This was before General Howard had entered the town and before General Reynolds' death—at least before General Howard knew of it. But General Howard had not seen General

Reynolds that morning, and General Reynolds had not passed over this field until that morning. It would appear then that General Reynolds did not indicate to General Howard the immediate field finally chosen for the battle.

Cemetery Hill

General Howard's force was very small, and when he retired to the hill and ridge he sought a position where he could resist or check the advance of the enemy, and this position the hill afforded him. The position was selected by him to meet a temporary and pressing emergency, and not especially, as I believe, with the view of its becoming a prominent point in the line of battle, in which the two entire armies were to be engaged. Cemetery Hill, with its flanks unprotected, is not a fit site for a battle-field. It was only made so by the troops which came upon the field later extending the flanks of General Howard's line along the ridge to the high hills at the extremity of either flank. At the time the general retired to the hill he had only a hope that the army could be brought to his aid in time to hold this line. The fact that the selection of the hill was to meet an emergency only, will be shown by a conversation between General Howard and myself soon after the troops were in position on the hill. The general said, in substance, to me: "We shall be attacked here this evening or early in the morning by General Lee's entire army. No troops are near enough to help us this evening, and I fear there will not be in the morning. If the enemy attacks in force before we get help we shall be wiped out of existence, as the enemy has already developed strength enough to convince me that his army is here. I shall fight as long as my command lasts and cripple the enemy as much as possible. I can do the enemy much damage. To cripple him as much as possible is the only way in which we can now help our army. I will not retreat." He then asked a few pertinent questions about the artillery. The subject was not again mentioned, and the enemy did not attack that evening or early the next morning. But this incident, in connection with the battle of the first day, shows how and under what circumstances Cemetery Hill and the flanking ridge was selected for the battle-field. As I understand, this is about General Howard's claim in this matter. As to the vicinity of Gettysburg being a good strategic point to bring on a general engagement with the enemy, I understood then, and I learned since, was conceded by all our leading military men.

The immediate hill and ridge on which our line of battle was in position, is what I speak of. This was selected by General Howard in the manner and for the purpose I have indicated, and not otherwise by anyone. Upon the arrival of General Hancock, and subsequently by General Meade, the Cemetery Hill and Ridge was decided upon as the line upon which to fight the army of General Lee.

The Position of the Artillery

As we were taking position on the hill, General Howard directed Colonel Wainwright, Chief of Artillery of the First Corps, and the colonel of the First New York Light Artillery to take charge of all the artillery on Cemetery Hill east of the Baltimore pike, and myself all the artillery on Cemetery Hill west of the same road. This order was not changed. Two batteries, however, were drawn from the First corps and placed on Cemetery Hill with those of the Eleventh corps under my command during the remainder of the first day.[4] My batteries were now in position commanding a portion of the streets of Gettysburg and the plain west of the hill. Colonel Wainwright's batteries commanded a portion of the streets and the plain east of the hill. The infantry were lying mainly in front of the batteries on the west, north and east of the hill. The troops in my front were in two lines, the most advanced being at the fence at the foot of the hill and next the Emmitsburg road. Our position was, in every sense, a good one, excepting that portion of the hill next the Baltimore pike and adjoining the city. Here the houses afforded good cover for the enemy's sharpshooters. The enemy made no more attacks during the evening or night. Our pickets were well out in front and the troops slept well after their hard day's work. At dawn on the morning of the 2d I saw General Meade, with General Howard, on the crest of the hill, studying the field. Several of the remaining corps were in the immediate neighborhood, and the feeling of the command was much better than it had been the evening before. The enemy, until sunrise, was quiet, except a scattering picket fire along the line. Back of us and a little to the right was the ravine made by Rock Creek and Culp's Hill. This was afterward filled by the Twelfth corps, and through this ravine General Ewell attempted to break later in the day. Before sunrise, and till some time after, this pass to our rear was not covered by our troops, and the infantry was not immediately at hand to do it. I therefore drew out from the batteries on the hill two six-gun batteries, and moving them to the rear of the hill and east of it, and half a mile from the entrance to the ravine, distributed them in sections over a half mile front, so their fire might be concentrated in the mouth of the pass. I felt confident, if the enemy should attempt to break through at that point, I could, with these twelve guns, hold the head of the column until the infantry could be brought up and take them in hand.

About sunrise General Hunt, Chief of Artillery of the army, came upon the hill to inspect the batteries and their positions. I had with me on the morning of the 2d Captain Wheeler, Thirteenth New York Independent Battery; Captain Wiedrich, Battery M [I], First New York Light Artillery; Captain Heckman, Battery H [K], First Ohio Artillery; Captain Dilger, Battery G [I], First Illinois [Ohio] Artillery, and Lieutenant Wilkeson [Bancroft], Battery G, Fourth United States Artillery.[5] These five batteries composed the artillery brigade of the Eleventh corps. The two batteries belonging to the First corps, which were with me on the evening of the 1st, had reported to their own chief on the east of the Baltimore pike. General Hunt, having made his inspection, said he was satisfied with my command and its disposition, and left without giving me any orders or instructions. Just at sunrise a battery of the enemy opened on us from the right and continued to fire for an hour. It was answered by Colonel Wainwright's batteries on the east of the Baltimore pike. Though several shells fell among my batteries, I did not reply. While this fire was progressing the pickets opened a sharp fire all along the eastern front of the field. After this battery had ceased firing the field was quiet until four o'clock in the afternoon. The interval was improved by each army commander in getting their respective armies in position for work—General Meade to hold his line and General Lee to break it. We could see large masses of the enemy's infantry moving to the right and left, leaving his centre comparatively bare of troops, and the batteries taking position along the entire face of the ridge which his lines occupied.

An Artillery Duel

At four o'clock the enemy opened their fire upon us from batteries distributed along at least a mile and a half of front, concentrating it upon Cemetery Hill. General Hunt says: "There were a hundred and twenty guns brought to bear upon our position. In general the enemy's fire or aim was not good. The line of fire was generally correct, but their elevation, in a majority of the shots, was little high, from two to twelve feet above our heads. Some shells fell short and many fell among us doing much damage, but not as much as they should have done if the fire had been correct." General Howard speaks of one shell which killed twenty-seven men in an infantry regiment. But the fire, on the whole, for so large a number of guns, was not good. I had, during this artillery duel, twenty-eight guns, and I presume Colonel Wainwright, on the east of the Baltimore pike, had the same number. My command received nearly all of this concentrated fire from this one hundred and twenty guns of the enemy.

One correspondent,[6] who was on the hill, speaks of the opening of this fire in this way: "Then came a storm of shot and shell; marble slabs were broken, iron fences shattered, horses disemboweled. The air was full of wild, hideous noises—the low buzz of round shot, the whizzing of elongated balls and the stunning explosion of shells overhead and all around." In speaking of our opening fire he says: "In three minutes the earth shook with the tremendous concussion of two hundred pieces of artillery." A correspondent writing from the position of General Sickles' corps, says: "He (General Lee) then began a heavy fire on Cemetery Hill. It must not be thought that this wrathful fire was unanswered. Our artillery began to play in a few moments, and hurled back defiance and like destruction on the rebel lines. Until 6 o'clock the roar of cannon, the rush of missiles and the bursting of bombs filled all the air. The clangor alone of this awful combat might well have confused and awed a less cool and watchful commander than General Meade." It was doubtless General Lee's intention to drive the artillery from the hill, both in aid of General Longstreet's attack on General Sickles and preparatory to the attack of General Ewell, made later in the day on our right. If this was the end in view, the artillery attack was useless, as no impression was made on the artillery beyond the loss of a very few men killed and wounded, a few horses killed and a caisson or two blown up. The batteries were in no way crippled or the men demoralized. The effect of our fire was watched and determined—as was usually done in artillery contests by the accuracy of the fire of the enemy. If our fire was bad, the enemy in a few minutes would get our range and hold it, but if our fire was accurate, we could determine the fact by the bad range of our adversaries. In this case the enemy fired much more rapidly than we, and with but comparatively little effect. We therefore concluded our fire was much more accurate and effective. This was shown to have been true by an inspection of the field after the battle. We also accomplished two other results by this fire. We held the fire of the enemy's guns to ourselves, where it was doing comparatively little damage and kept it from being turned upon our infantry, where it would have done material injury. We also compelled them to exhaust their ammunition, which to us was of importance. We believed we had more than they, and if we could draw theirs from them the final result would be in our favor.

Longstreet's Advance

This fire continued three quarters of an hour and then ceased nearly altogether for a few moments. It then opened again with increased violence as General Longstreet moved against General Sickles' corps and became engaged. During the two hours this fierce battle progressed between General Longstreet's and General Sickles' corps, the artillery duel progressed between the enemy's batteries scattered along the enemy's line and our batteries on Cemetery Hill. The enemy's fire from guns distributed over two miles of front was concentrated on the little patch of ground we occupied, while the lines of fire from our several batteries spread out like a fan to meet the fire of each battery in our front. The batteries under the command of Colonel Wainwright were no more idle than those under my command. He was a most gallant officer and an accomplished artillerist. And here pardon me if I give expression to a little feeling of pride for the battery I brought into the service from Jefferson and St. Lawrence counties, N.Y.—Battery D, First New York Light Artillery, commanded by Captain George B. Winslow. I had left this battery, as its captain, but a few weeks before and had had for my first lieutenant the then captain. It belonged to the Third corps and fought with it in this battle. General Howard in his review of the battle in the *Atlantic Monthly* for July, 1876, but making the mistake of writing *Bigelow* for *Winslow*, doubtless owing to the similarity in the pronunciation, says: "Sickles' batteries here did wonderfully effective service. Winslow fired rapidly from a position near A. Trostle's barn, and when forced to retire did so with the prolonge, keeping up the fire.[7] The

Confederates, pressing back the broken infantry line, came upon this battery with a rush. Winslow is said to have blown them from the muzzles of his guns, but still they came on and clambered over his limbers and shot his horses. Five of his non-commissioned officers and twenty-two of his men were either killed or wounded and he himself wounded in the side. Still he held on and fired till the corps chief of artillery, Mr. Gilvery, had brought up his reserve battery to the high ground in his rear." It was this battery—when General Meade, just previous to the battle of the Wilderness, called for the reports of all the battles the regiments and batteries had been engaged in that they might have them inscribed on their flags—bore off the palm. It had been engaged in more battles than any other battery or any regiment in the Army of the Potomac.

The Hill Assaulted

At eight o'clock in the evening General Ewell made an attack on our line from Cemetery Hill, extending around to our extreme right. The extreme right of the assaulting line was at the present site of the keeper's house of the National Cemetery. The charge on the hill was very severe and with the extreme right of the line the enemy ran over Wiedrich's battery. At this point they had advanced close to our line under cover of the houses and the battery could give but a few shots before the infantry was forced back and the battery in the enemy's possession. When the artillerymen could work their guns no longer, and the enemy was among them, Wiedrich's men defended the guns with handspikes, rammers and every other thing they could use. But, of course, to no purpose, except the capture of one officer and several brave men. As soon as proper disposition could be made of the infantry and the enemy driven again into the town, Captain Wiedrich took possession of the battery and did good work with it on the retreating column. By reason of our infantry being between our other batteries and the enemy we were not able to use our guns. The fighting on our right, about Culp's Hill, was heavy for a little while. Colonel Wainwright had better opportunities to use his batteries than I and he used them effectively in repulsing this advance of the enemy. The night was quiet, excepting for a few minutes at 2 A.M., when the enemy opened a rapid fire on us from the batteries west of my position. I replied for a few moments only, when I ordered the firing to cease and the men to lie down again for sleep. The enemy's fire soon ceased and we rested till morning, sleeping well, for we were very tired. At daylight on the morning of the 3d the battle was renewed with great vigor from East Cemetery Hill all along the line to our extreme right. General Ewell had gained some advantage on the evening of the 2d on this front, when our line had been weakened to reinforce our left and resist General Longstreet's attack. This fight was initiated by our troops, under the immediate command of General Slocum, to re-establish our line by driving General Ewell back to the line he held before his attack of the evening previous. The fighting on this front was very severe and lasted five hours, when the enemy's line having been forced back, ours was re-established and the fighting ceased. None of the guns of my command could be made available in this morning's fighting. Colonel Wainwright's command, east of the Baltimore pike, was very active through it all.

Preparing For Fire

At 10 o'clock the field again became quiet and continued so till 1 o'clock in the afternoon. During this period of quiet aides from General Meade's headquarters informed us that General Lee was massing his infantry heavily against our left, while his batteries remained distributed along the line he had held since the first day. General Hunt was several times on the hill and said, from information gathered, he had reached the conclusion the enemy would concentrate his artillery fire on Cemetery Hill with the view of dislodging our artillery and then move against our left with the intention of breaking our line. If his conclusions should prove correct the position I held would be the one upon which the enemy would open, and my command would suffer most. He wished me to exercise my own judgment as to how many batteries I could use to advantage, and to draw them, together with all the ammunition I might need, from the reserve without further orders. I anticipated rough work and got my men in as good condition as possible and the batteries were ready for work. I had concluded the question to be settled with me would be whether my command could be driven from the hill. I did not fear this, but I did fear that my men would not last long enough to do all that we ought to do in the then coming contest. I was fully aware of the fearful effects of artillery fire when concentrated from a superior number of guns distributed on a long line and concentrated upon a single point. I had experienced it from the enemy and practised it upon them before that day and very well knew its effects. I was now to experience it more severely by many fold than ever before. At this time I had five batteries on the hill belonging to the corps.[8] In preparation for the expected attack I drew two from the reserve. These were Battery H, First United States Artillery, Lieutenant Eakin commanding, and Captain Taft's Fifth New York Independent Battery. These seven batteries faced west, commanding the plain and the low hills beyond. The right battery, Captain Wiedrich, was just in rear or east of where the keeper's house now stands, the left battery. Lieutenant Eakin, on the point of the hill close to the little grove of old trees south of the Cemetery. The line of batteries followed the crest of the hill between the two flank batteries. Nearly all the guns and all the caissons were among the graves. Each battery was in position as in park—fourteen feet between the guns—the limbers and caissons at proper distances in rear of the guns. The horses were hitched to the carriages and the men were standing or lying near their post as at rest on parade. The ammunition chests had been filled. The spaces between the batteries were greater than the spaces between the guns of any one battery, but yet they were close together. No earthworks were thrown up to protect the men, nor could there have been without digging up the dead in the Cemetery. We were in plain view of the batteries of the enemy on at least a mile and a half of his line. The slope of the hill in our rear was too steep to use as a cover for the guns or even the caissons. The distance of the enemy's guns from us was from three-fourths of a mile to a mile and a half. An excellent range, the country all open, no woods intervening between the line or between the enemy's batteries and Cemetery Hill. We made the best target for artillery practice the enemy had during the war. But there was another side to it. We commanded their guns as well as they did ours, with the advantage on the enemy's part of being more scattered. In addition to this we commanded the plain perfectly, with no timber intervening, over which the enemy's infantry must advance to the charge.

The Ball Opened

At 1 o'clock in the afternoon a Whitworth gun was fired from Seminary Hill, the shot passing low over our heads. This was the signal gun, at the firing of which all the artillery of the enemy was to open. In a minute or two every battery on the whole line in our front had opened, concentrating the fire mainly on Cemetery Hill. Of the number of the guns employed at this time by the enemy, Colonel James C. Biddle,[9] in his article, "General Meade at Gettysburg," says: "Suddenly the enemy opened upon us a terrific artillery fire with not less than one hundred and twenty-five guns. Our batteries, which had been posted by General Hunt, the efficient chief of artillery, replied with about seventy guns—the nature of the ground not admitting of the use of more." The firing was rapid. I estimated at the time at least one shot a minute for each gun, and this rapid firing was sustained throughout this artillery contest. Much of the time, however, the firing was much more rapid. From the fire on our west front, Colonel Wainwright's batteries, on East Cemetery Hill, were covered by the town and the nature of the ground, the batteries under my command receiving nearly the entire fire. The enemy had no sooner got to work than my batteries replied with energy, and, judging by the usual methods of determining the effects of artillery fire with good results, the men were persistently cool and showed no indications of demoralization. When there was no longer a doubt but the enemy intended and expected to drive us from the hill and force us to seek cover, I drew several batteries from the reserve artillery of the army, and placed them in the line on the crest of the hill, between the batteries already there. The batteries at this time in line were as close together as I thought advisable, or precedent to place them. I have now no memoranda of what batteries I drew from the reserve after the firing began, or how many of them there were. When the battle was over these batteries returned to their command and were with me only two or three hours during the heat of the battle. All orders given to them were verbal. Belonging to my command were twenty-eight guns; in Eakin's and Taft's batteries ten guns; in all thirty-eight. I drew from the reserve during the firing sufficient to make the whole number on Cemetery Hill and west of the Baltimore pike a little over sixty guns—the exact number I do not remember.[10]

  The enemy was now doing us a good deal of damage; but, as the day before, the line of fire was perfect, the average elevation a little high. The majority of the shells passed over us but very low down, so close to our heads and reaching us so rapidly, I ordered all my own officers to dismount from their horses and all other officers who had occasion to come upon the hill were directed to dismount when they came to the line of the batteries. But many, very many, shells and solid shot fell among the batteries and many shells exploded just in front of them, the fragments scattering among the men and horses. The fire from our west front had progressed fifteen or twenty minutes, when several guns, two batteries or more, opened on us from the ridge beyond East Cemetery Hill. The line of fire from these last batteries and the line of fire from the batteries on our west front were such as to leave the town between the two lines of fire. These last guns opened directly on the right flank of my line of batteries. The gunners got our range at almost the first shot. Passing low over Colonel Wainwright's guns they caught us square in flank and with the elevation perfect. It was admirable shooting. They raked the whole line of batteries, killed and wounded the men and horses and blew up the caissons rapidly. I saw one shell go through six horses standing broadside. To meet this new fire I drew from the batteries facing west the 20 pound Parrott battery of Captain Taft, and wheeling it half round to the right brought it to bear on them. I also drew from the reserve one battery and placed it in position on Taft's right. The hill at this point is so narrow—by the way, the widest part of the ridge on the hill—that these guns were as close together as they could be worked, and even then, to get a standing place, they were placed by sections en echelon with the left advanced. These guns were at the Indian monument.[11]

Meade On The Field

Fortunately for us these batteries, placed in the new line, at once secured the exact range of their immediate adversaries. In a few minutes the enemy's fire almost ceased, and when it again opened, and while the fire was progressing, it was irregular and wild. They did not again get our range as they had it before we replied, but continued to fire wild until the close of the battle, doing us but little more damage. I learned from officers who, after the battle, visited the ground occupied by these batteries of the enemy, that the dead men and horses and broken carriages showed they had suffered very severely from our fire. While the fire was at its greatest severity General Meade, accompanied by a staff officer, came on the hill and asked me if we could stay. I assured him we would do so. He said the result of the fight depended on our holding the hill. I replied that the enemy also seemed to have the same idea. He offered no criticism as to the disposition of the batteries, nor did he give me any orders. He appeared to be much concerned as to the possibility of holding the men up to the work under the fire then going on. He remained only two or three minutes, but repeated the question: "Can you stay here?" and: "Are your men thoroughly in hand?" I replied: "The officers and men were in good condition and we would stay." But it was a fearful fire the enemy were pouring into us and it was not surprising that he was anxious. This was the first and last since I ever saw General Meade while a battle was in progress. He appeared at that time to be perfectly cool and collected in his judgment, but in his manner excited and nervous. All he said was to the point, and showed a full appreciation of everything about him, even to the details of my own work. Still his movements and manner of address showed a nervous and excited condition of mind and body. General Sumner was the only other prominent general I ever saw who showed this same high nervous condition in battle. I have been in battle where I could study the characteristics of Generals Grant, Sherman, Sheridan, Hooker, Heintzelman, Richardson, Sedgwick, Thomas, Sickles, Howard, and many others of our prominent generals, and all, except the two named were intensely cool and composed, no matter how great the pressure of battle nor how great the personal danger. But in none have I seen a cooler exhibition of judgment than in Generals Meade and Sumner and this while exercised under apparently great mental and physical excitement.

Nothing which can be written will convey to the non-military man the slightest idea of the fire concentrated on Cemetery Hill during the hour and a half it continued. The shells must have reached us at the rate of one hundred and upwards a minute at the least. The area covered by the batteries was very small, only about one-half of the surface of an ordinary village burying- ground. All of the slope of Cemetery Hill, which has since become the National Cemetery, and in front of it to the Emmitsburg road, we did not occupy. The infantry was so disposed as to give them good cover. The enemy turned their attention exclusively to the batteries on the crest of the hill. The enemy's fire was a little high, the majority of the shells passing low or close down over our heads. Yet an immense number were well directed and dropped into our batteries, doing much damage. The officers, men and horses were killed and wounded rapidly. A caisson was blown up every few minutes, and now and then an artillery carriage was struck and knocked to pieces. Two of our guns exploded. Our own batteries did good work, and with the exception of those guns which had either exploded or were knocked off their carriages, not a single one ceased its work. The officers and men were cool, and secured the exact range and elevation of the enemy's batteries. The accuracy of our fire could be determined by the field-glasses and the effect on the enemy by reducing the accuracy of their fire or compelling them to fire wild. We did not expect, or even hope, to silence the batteries of the enemy. From their scattered positions and extended line it was a military impossibility to do so. We did what we could to injure them and lessen the serious effects of their fire upon us by compelling them to fire recklessly. We accomplished this and held our position on the hill without any gun ceasing fire unless it was disabled. The men showed no signs of demoralization.

A Terrific Cannonade

Of this fire General Howard, in his article before referred to, says: "The signal gun was fired by the enemy, and from the southwest, west, north and northeast, his batteries opened, hurling into the Cemetery grounds missiles of every description. Shells burst in the air, on the ground, at our right and left, and in front, killing men and horses, exploding caissons, over turning tombstones and smashing fences. The troops hugged their cover, when they had any, as well as they could. One regiment of Steinwehr's was fearfully cut to pieces with a shell. Several officers, passing a certain path within a stone's throw of my position, were either killed or wounded.... Men fell while eating, or while their food was in their hands, and some with cigars in their mouths. As there seemed to be actually no place of safety, my staff officers sat by me nearly in front of four twenty-pound Parrott guns that played over our heads, almost every available space being covered with artillery." Colonel James C. Biddle, in the article on "General Meade at Gettysburg," says: "This artillery duel, which lasted an hour and a half, was the most severe of any experienced anywhere during the war. The air was filled with bursting shell and solid shot, and the very earth shook with resounding cannon. General Meade well understood that the object of the enemy in this fire was to demoralize our men, preparatory to making a grand assault." Colonel W.H. Taylor, of General Lee's staff, in his "Campaign in Pennsylvania," says: "After a heavy artillery fire along the entire line and at a given signal the movement began." In the same article Captain

Louis G. Young, of General Pettigrew's staff says: "On the morning of the 3d of July General Pettigrew, commanding Heth's division, was instructed to report to General Longstreet, who directed him to form in the rear of Pickett's division and support his advance on Cemetery Hill, which would be commenced as soon as the fire from our artillery should have driven the enemy from his guns and prepared the way for the attack." General Longstreet, in his article, "Lee in Pennsylvania," says: "The cannonading, which opened along both lines, was grand."

Letting The Enemy Out

While the fire was progressing and was at its greatest height, General Hunt came on the hill. We, General Howard and myself, were standing near the Indian Monument canvassing the situation. General Hunt said General Meade was satisfied the enemy's infantry were heavily massed against our left and he was making a desperate effort to silence the artillery on Cemetery Hill, preparatory to making an assault on our left. I asked General Hunt if General Meade considered an assault by the enemy desirable. He replied "General Meade had expressed a hope that the enemy would attack, and he had no fear of the result." I said: "If this is so, why not let them out while we are all in good condition. I would cease firing at once and the enemy could reach but one conclusion, that of our being driven from the hill." I asked him to see General Meade and get permission to cease firing and wait developments. General Hunt asked, with an expression of anxiety, if I could control my men if I should cease firing while the fire of the enemy was so heavy. I told him: "The men were under perfect control by their officers and nothing was to be feared from the order." General Howard said: "My suggestion was a good one and, if put into execution, would produce the desired result. If the enemy intended to attack they would then do it at once, and if they did not intend to do so we should know that fact." After a few moments conversation with General Howard, General Hunt said he would not wait to see General Meade, but give the order at once himself. On his way to General Meade's headquarters he would order the batteries on my left to cease firing and report what he had done to General Meade when he should reach him. General Howard concurred in the plan and advised General Hunt, as an officer of the army staff, to give the order. General Hunt, as Chief of Artillery of the army, gave the order and was responsible for it, I only for the suggestion and the expression of my views as to what would be the result. No other officers were present during the conversation. I speak especially of this order and these incidents, because of the effect the order and compliance with it by the artillery had upon the enemy, and the marvelous results which followed it in deciding the battle. I do not believe the final charge would have been made, as it was made, if this order had not been given.

General Hunt then left me to give the order to the batteries on my left. I commenced with the battery on my right, walked the whole length of my line, giving each battery in succession orders to cease firing and officers and men to lie down and cover themselves from the enemy's fire was well as possible until the enemy's fire had ceased, then to be ready at once for any emergency. General Hunt rode rapidly down the line to General Meade's headquarters, ordering the batteries on my left to cease firing. In ten minutes from the time it was determined to give the order, the batteries from my right to General Meade's headquarters had ceased firing. In a few moments more the order had been sent to Round Top along the line and the firing had ceased over our entire front. Almost immediately the enemy ceased their fire and a singularly depressing quiet covered the entire field. But this quiet was to last for a few minutes only. I do not think it was more than ten minutes after the artillery fire had ceased before the enemy appeared in line of battle, advancing in line of two brigades front, over the ridge in front of the left centre of our army. The description of this magnificent charge, probably the most magnificent charge ever made by an army, has been repeated and read many times. I only speak of the artillery on the hill and the part it bore in these operations. Beyond that, I will not attempt to give details. So soon as the enemy's first line of battle had fully developed by advancing over the ridge, I ordered all the batteries facing the west to open on it, the batteries facing the northeast to open again on the artillery beyond East Cemetery Hill. So far as I remember, not a single battery, save perhaps one in the left wing of our army, had been so crippled that it was not fully effective. Those under my command were capable of and did full work.

The Advance

When the enemy first appeared advancing over the ridge the range for the guns on the hill was long. I therefore directed the brass guns to use solid shot and the rifle guns to use percussion shell. This order was changed when necessary, as the enemy advanced and came nearer our line. When the first line of the enemy had advanced about two hundred paces in front of the ridge a second line, in every way similar to the first, followed, moving at the same step as the advanced line. The enemy's lines of battle were now in plain view, no trees or other obstructions intervening. By watching the effects of the fire the men very soon secured the exact range of the two lines of battle and held it. Each solid shot or unexploded shell which struck either line cut out two men, but when a shell exploded immediately in front of either line it cut out four, six, eight, or even more men, making a wide gap in their line. These gaps and the width of them could be as distinctly seen from the hill as if we had been close to them. By this guide, and watching the explosion of the shells, the men estimated very accurately on the effects of their fire and were able to keep the range of the enemy as the two lines moved toward our line of battle. When the enemy had passed over about one-third of the distance between the ridge and our line both lines halted, faced to the right and left on their centres, closed their ranks, which had been depleted by the artillery fire, dressed their line and moved on. This was done under as galling an artillery fire as infantry was ever subjected to. This they did again when about another third of the distance between the ridge and our line had been covered. In each of the halts and closing up of the ranks of the two lines they were very materially shortened. The artillery fire up to this time had told terribly on them. Until the enemy's ranks had been closed the second time and the lines dressed they had only been exposed to artillery fire, the infantry not yet being able to reach them with their musketry fire. Until the enemy had reached the point of the second alignment the men had moved at a quick step only, but from this point they moved at a double quick and were soon covered by the intervening ground from the guns on Cemetery Hill.

The Repulse

We, on the hill, saw no more of them until after they had struck our line and their final repulse had been secured. The men were then, when brought again under the fire from the guns on the hill, in full retreat and each man making the best of his way back to the cover of the ridge, over which they had advanced when they commenced the charge. In this retreat there were no two men together, but each man was running by himself to gain the cover of the hills within his own lines. As they appeared to us, from the cover of the intervening ground, the artillery on the hill was all again turned on them. While to them this last fire was doubtless very demoralizing, yet I do not think the damage done could have been great. They were too much scattered to make the fire, from artillery effective. Colonel W.W. Wood,[12] of Virginia, who was with Pickett's Division and participated in the final charge, says that the brigade, regimental and line officers of the division received orders, before the artillery of the enemy opened, that when his artillery should have silenced ours that the line should move to the charge without further orders; that in compliance with these instructions, when our fire ceased, the division did move without additional orders being sent along the line. He and all other officers believed our guns had been silenced and driven from our position. He, then a captain, got his company ready and moved without further orders.

General Howard says of this charge and the work of the artillery: "At half-past 2 P.M. we ceased to reply. We had ammunition and were not silenced, but we knew this cannonade preceded an attack, and we thought it possible the enemy would conclude that we had been stopped by their effective shots and would proceed to the contemplated assault; then we should need batteries in readiness and plenty of ammunition. We were right. The firing of the enemy lulled, and I could see, better than the day before, their infantry in line; at least a quarter of a mile of it was exposed to my view as it started from Oak Ridge, opposite our left. It was like an extensive parade; the flags were flying and the lines steadily advancing. As I now know, these were Pickett's and Pettigrew's divisions and part of Anderson's. On they came. As soon as they were near enough Osborn, Wainwright, McGilvery [13] and other artillery chiefs started the fire of their batteries—first with solid shot, making hardly any impression, soon with shells exploding near and over and beyond the advancing lines. Now gaps were plainly made, but quickly filled. When nearer the canister was freely used and the gaps in the enemy's lines grew bigger and harder to close." Col. Biddle says: "Soon Lee's attacking column, composed of Pickett's division, supported by Wilcox and Pettigrew, made a most gallant and well-sustained assault on our lines, advancing steadily, under a heavy artillery fire from the guns Lee thought he had silenced, to within musket range of our infantry." Colonel Taylor, of General Lee's staff, says: "The enemy's batteries soon opened upon our lines with canister and the left seemed to stagger under it, but the advance was resumed with some degree of steadiness. Pickett's troops did not appear to be checked by the batteries and only halted to deliver a fire when close under musket-range. . . . The charge was made down a gentle slope and then up to the enemy's lines, a distance of over half a mile, denuded of forests and in full sight of the enemy and perfect range of their artillery." General Longstreet says: "As they (Pickett's division) started up the ridge over one hundred cannon from the breastworks of the Federals hurled a rain of canister, grape and shell down upon them. Still they pressed on, till half-way up the slope, when the crest of the hill was lit up with a solid sheet of flame, as the masses of infantry rose and fired. When the smoke cleared away Pickett's division was gone. Nearly two-thirds of his men lay dead on the field and the survivors were sullenly retreating down the hill. Mortal man could not have stood that fire. In half an hour the contested field was cleared and the battle of Gettysburg was over." On a subsequent occasion General Lee said to General Longstreet: "General, why didn't you stop all that thing that day?"

The End Of The Battle

During all the time we were giving our attention exclusively to the enemy's infantry, the guns of the enemy on the ridge opposite were pouring a rapid and well-directed fire into our batteries on the hill. All their guns were opened on us, and as we did not reply, except to the guns beyond East Cemetery Hill, they improved the opportunity to get our exact range at their leisure, and they did it. Their fire was exceedingly harassing and did us much damage. Several times my men swung their guns around to answer the fire of the enemy's batteries, which were annoying them so severely. I was as often compelled to order them to turn their fire back upon the enemy's infantry, where their work would tell most effectively in deciding the fate of the day. It was hard for my men to have this fire concentrated on them from half the enemy's line, while they were not permitted to reply. The effects of long discipline in the field, and the obstinacy of veteran troops, were put to their utmost test, while more than a hundred guns were playing on them, manned by as old and skilled artillerists as themselves. Yet they were not permitted to reply, but ordered to direct their fire upon a body of troops in no way annoying them at the time. When those of the enemy's infantry who were neither killed, wounded or captured had reached the cover of the hills, in the enemy's line, their batteries ceased firing. We ceased firing and the battle was over.

I have endeavored, in this article, to give nothing except what the artillery under my immediate command did in this battle. It necessarily performed a very important part in the three days' fighting. I have not intended to convey the idea that the artillery of the other corps did not do as well, or perhaps even better than we. The position in the line held by the Eleventh corps, the topography of the battle-field and the plan of General Lee, in fighting this battle, necessitated the heavy artillery attacks of the second and third days upon the hill, and as equally necessitated our holding it and removing them, no matter what the loss might have been in men and materiel. I do know the two batteries to our immediate left and front suffered much more severely than any batteries under my command; that they and other batteries in the line did their work as well as we, I have no doubt. I did not leave my command at any time during the battle, and consequently am not familiar with the work of other artillery than my own. It may be noticed that I have said comparatively little about orders received, and have spoken of myself as responsible for much of the work of the batteries. I received no orders from any source after we had taken position on Cemetery Hill on the first day of the battle, except as General Howard or General Hunt gave me instructions to call for batteries and ammunition and the several phases of the battle to use my own discretion in using the artillery. My position was not changed after four o'clock the first day till the close of the battle. General Howard was in the immediate vicinity all the time and of course kept his eye on my work; but, as he gave me no orders, I assume he was satisfied with it. The change of the direction of the fire, to command different parts of the field, was all the maneuvering we did. This I did as occasion demanded. The number of additional batteries required to hold the hill and do the necessary work I drew from the reserve artillery of the army as occasion required.

The Losses of the Artillery

On the morning of the 4th I found I had lost a little more than one hundred horses in the five batteries which belonged to the corps. To move the artillery with the corps I required one hundred new horses. The Quartermaster's Department of the army had no horses for us. We were ordered to be ready to move on the morning of the 5th. I therefore sent out detachments of my men on the morning of the 4th and impressed from the citizens in the vicinity of Gettysburg the one hundred horses required. These horses were afterward paid for by the Corps Quartermaster, General Le Duc, the present Commissioner of Agriculture. Immediately after the battle the batteries drawn from the reserve were ordered to report again to their command. I do not know how the horses they lost were replaced. They lost many.

I have not the necessary data at hand to state the number of killed and wounded or the loss of materiel in my command during the three days of the battle.

Notes

[1] Wheeler and Dilger were to the left of the Carlisle Road, Wilkeson to the right with Barlow. Heckman was initially held in reserve.

[2] Both Corps withdrew at approximately the same time in what most have described as a less-than-orderly retreat.

[3] Colonel Meysenberg was General Howard's adjutant-general.

[4] Hall's Second Maine Battery was one of the "two batteries" of which Osborn speaks. He may have been mistaken about there being two batteries.

[5] Trusting his memory rather than his battle report, Osborn is guilty of careless errors of identification.

[6] Charles Carleton Coffin was the correspondent quoted by Osborn.

[7] Osborn is mistaken. Winslow fought in the Wheatfield, Bigelow near A. Trostle's barn.

[8] There were three Eleventh Corps batteries in the cemetery; Heckman had been retired to the rear and Wiedrich, on East Cemetery Hill, faced northeast. Osborn drew five batteries from the Artillery Reserve.

[9] Colonel James C. Biddle served on General Meade's staff.

[10] Osborn's estimate is high; See Appendix A.

[11] Osborn does not identify this reserve battery. His description of its location from the official records as, "in the rear of and perpendicular to Wheeler," places it near the center of Evergreen Cemetery on high ground in line with the Soldiers' National Monument, in an area now occupied by a small mausoleum. Wheeler's battery location to the left of Bancroft is not presently marked, but was near the center of Osborn's line, facing Seminary Ridge.

[12] Capt. William Walter Wood served with Company G, Fourteenth Virginia Regiment of Pickett's Division.

[13] Lt. Col. Freeman McGilvery commanded the First Brigade of the Artillery Reserve. The 49 guns under his command extended from the George Weikert Lane north to the Second Corps Artillery positions in the area that was the objective of the Confederate assault.

Appendix C

Report of Capt. William H. McCartney,
First Massachusetts Battery,
Artillery Brigade, Sixth Army Corps.

Editor's Note: *The report of William H. McCartney, First Massachusetts Battery, seems to confirm Osborn's insignificant but interesting anecdote of the jettisoned ammunition. Captain McCartney seems to infer that Edgell's First New Hampshire Battery, "said to have been out of ammunition," and relieved by McCartney for that reason, was the battery that left 48 unspent rounds "near the position." Osborn points the finger at Norton's Ohio Battery, whom Edgell had relieved earlier. The present location of Edgell's battery in the National Cemetery is a considerable distance in front of Norton's Battery H, First Ohio Light Artillery. This may be because there was not room to place both batteries in the original position which they both occupied at different times. Both batteries fired 3-inch projectiles.*

Camp of Battery A, Massachusetts Artillery,
July 11, 1863.

Sir: I have the honor to report that on the 3d day of July, current, this command was ordered into position on the left of the cemetery near Gettysburg, by Major Osborn, chief of artillery Eleventh Corps, to relieve the First New Hampshire Battery, said to have been out of ammunition.

I have also the honor to report that I caused to be collected, from a piece of woods directly in rear of the ground which had been occupied by said First New Hampshire Battery, 48 rounds of 3-inch projectiles, perfect; 22 rounds having been found near the position which had been occupied by one limber.

I am, sir, with very much respect,

W. H. McCartney,
Captain, Commanding.

Capt. A.E. King,
Assistant Adjutant-General.

Appendix D

Thomas Ward Osborn (1833 - 1898)

Thomas Ward Osborn was born on March 9, 1833* in Scotch Plains, Union County, New Jersey and died at the home of his nephew, Dr. Dwight L. Hubbard, in New York City on December 18, 1898 at 10 p.m. In 1842 his parents, Jonathan and Amelia Van Deeman Osborn, settled the family on a farm in North Wilna, Jefferson County, New York. He received his early education at Gouverneur Academy and was a member of the class of 1860 of Madison University (now Colgate University) in Hamilton, New York. He studied law with Starbuck and Sawyer in Watertown, New York and was admitted to the bar in 1861. That same year he entered the Union army as Lieutenant of Battery D, New York Light Artillery, rising eventually to the rank of Colonel. The principle campaigns in which he participated were the Peninsula, Fredericksburg, Chancellorsville, Gettysburg, Lookout Mountain, Chattanooga, Atlanta, Savannah and the Carolinas. At Gettysburg he commanded the Eleventh Corps Artillery and served as Chief of Artillery, Fourth Corps, and later Chief of Artillery of the Army and Department of the Tennessee during Sherman's campaign through Georgia and the Carolinas.

Following the war, Osborn was appointed assistant commissioner of the Bureau of Refugees and Freedmen for Florida (1865-1866). As a member of the Florida state constitutional convention he helped draft the state constitution in 1868. Following membership in the state senate, Osborn was elected as a Republican to the United States Senate, where he served from June 25, 1868 to March 3, 1873. In 1876 he was appointed by President Grant United States commissioner for the Centennial Exposition in Philadelphia, after which he moved to New York City and practiced law. Colonel Osborn is interred in Hillside Cemetery, North Adams, Berkshire County, Massachusetts.

*Although the Library of Congress Cataloging Authority Record and the Biographical Directory of the United States Congress list Thomas Ward Osborn's birth year as 1836, Colonel Osborn's personal papers in the Colgate University Archives indicate that he was born in 1833, not 1836. In addition, the cemetery records of North Adams, MA list him as died on December 18, 1898, age 65, and his gravestone in the Hillside Cemetery at North Adams confirms his birthdate as March 9, 1833.

—*W.Edmonston*

References

Primary Materials.

Osborn, Thomas Ward. Unpublished letters and papers. Hamilton, NY: Colgate University Archives.

Documents.

U.S. War Department (1880-1901) *The War of the Rebellion: A Compilation of Official Records of the Union and Confederate Armies.* 128 Vols. & Index. Washington, DC (See especially Vol. 27, Pp. 229-230, 232, 360, 727-728, 734, 747-758, 891-895.)

Newspapers and Articles.

Howard, O.O. (1876) Campaign and Battle of Gettysburg, June & July, 1863. *The Atlantic Monthly*, XXXVIII, 48-71.

Osborn, T.W. (May 31, 1879) The Artillery at Gettysburg. *Philadelphia Weekly Times.*

Schurz, C. (July, 1907) The Battle of Gettysburg. *McClune's Magazine*, XXVIX, 272-285.

Books.

Alexander, E.P. (1907) *Military Memoirs of a Confederate.* New York: Charles Scribner's Sons. (See especially Pp. 419, 427-428.)

Fox, W.F. (1902) *New York at Gettysburg.* 3 Vols. Albany, NY: J.B. Lyon Co. (See especially Vol. 3, Pp. 1194-1195.)

Gallagher, G.W. (Ed.) (1989) *Fighting for the Confederacy* by E.P. Alexander. Chapel Hill: University of North Carolina Press.

Howard, O.O. (1907) *Autobiography.* 2 Vols. New York: Baker & Taylor. (See especially Vol. 1, p. 422.)

Hunt, H.J. (1981) *Three Days at Gettysburg.* Golden, CO: Outbooks Reprint. (First appeared in *Century Magazine* and later in *Battles and Leaders of the Civil War.* (See especially p. 67, note 15.)

Johnson, R.V. & Buel, C.C. (Eds.) (1884-1889) *Battles and Leaders of the Civil War.* 4 Vols. New York: Century Co.

Nevins, A. (Ed.) (1962) *A Diary of Battle: The Personal Journals of Colonel Charles S. Wainwright, 1860-1865.* New York: Harcourt, Brace & World.(See especially Pp. 50-51, 55, 209, 245-246.)

Schurz, C. (1907-1908) *The Reminiscences of Carl Schurz.* 3 Vol. New York: The McClure Co.

Secondary Materials.

Coddington, E.B. (1963) *The Gettysburg Campaign: A Study in Command.* New York: Charles Scribner's Sons.

Downey, F. (1958) *The Guns at Gettysburg.* New York: David McKay Co.

Freeman, D.S. (1942-1944) *Lee's Lieutenants: A Study in Command.* 3 Vols. New York: Charles Scribner's Sons. (See especially Vol. 3, p. 186.)

Harwell, R. & Racine, P.N. (Eds.) (1986) *The Fiery Trail.* Knoxville: University of Tennessee Press.

Hassler, W.W. Jr. (1970) *Crisis at the Crossroads: The First Day at Gettysburg.* Tuscaloosa: University of Alabama Press.

Longacre, E.G. (1977) *The Man Behind the Guns.* Cranbury, NJ: A.S. Barnes & Co.

Naisawald, L.V.L. (1960) *Grape and Cannister: The Story of the Field Artillery in the Army of the Potomac, 1861-1865.* New York: Oxford University Press.

Stewart, G.R. (1980) *Pickett's Charge: A Microhistory of the Final Attack at Gettysburg, July 3, 1863.* Dayton, OH: Morningside Bookshop.

Wise, J.C. (1915) *The Long Arm of Lee: The History of the Artillery of the Army of Northern Virginia.* 2 Vols. New York: J.P. Bell Co.

Index
Experiences at the Battle of Gettysburg

Arrowsmith, George, Lieut. Col., 15
Artillery Reserve, 22, 32, 37, 40

Baltimore Pike, 15, 38
Bancroft, Lieut, 13, 15
Barlow, Francis C., Brig. Gen., 10, 13
Battery D, 1st NY Light Artillery, 24, 32
Bealeton VA., 8
Berry, Hiram, Gen., 36
Buffalo NY, 27
Buford, John, Brig. Gen., 18
Burnside, Ambrose E., Maj. Gen., 43

Casualties, Gettysburg, 8
Cemetery Hill, 9-10, 13, 15, 17-18, 21-23, 29
Century Magazine, 23
Chancellorsville, 32
Culpeper, VA, 8
Culp's Hill, 9, 13, 15, 17-18, 23

Dilger, Hubert, Capt, 7, 10
Doubleday, Abner, Maj. Gen., 9, 10

Early, Jubal A., Maj. Gen., 26-27, 29
Eleventh Corps, 7-9, 13, 15-17, 21, 23, 26-27
Emmitsburg, MD, 9
Ewell, Richard, Lieut. Gen., 8, 10, 18, 21-23, 25-26, 29

Fifth Corps, 8, 25
First Corps, 8-10, 13, 15, 17-19, 21, 23, 25, 29
Fort McAllister, GA, 43
Frederick, MD, 8
Fredericksburg, VA, 8, 24, 43

Gouverneur, NY, 24
Grant, Ulysses S., Lieut. Gen., 24
Griffith, Capt., 10

Hagerstown, MD, 45

Hancock, Winfield S., Maj. Gen., 19, 23, 27, 42-43
Harrisburg, PA, 8, 18
Heckman, Lewis, Capt., 7, 10, 13, 15
Heintzelman, Samuel P., Maj. Gen., 36
Hill, Ambrose P., Maj. Gen., 8, 23
Hooker, Joseph, Maj. Gen., 8-9, 36, 44
Howard, Oliver O., Maj. Gen., 7, 10, 13, 15-19, 21-23, 26-27, 31, 36-37, 39-40, 44
Hunt, Henry J., Brig. Gen., 22-23, 32, 37, 39-40

Jefferson County, NY, 24

Kennesaw Mountain, GA, 44

Lee, Robert E., Gen., 8-9, 15-18, 21, 23, 25, 29, 31-32, 39-40, 42-45
Lewis County, NY, 24
Little Round Top, 18
Longstreet, James, Lieut. Gen., 8, 23, 25
Lookout Mountain, TN, 44
Lutheran Seminary, 9

Malvern Hill, 43
Martinsburg, VA, 8
Meade, George G., Maj. Gen., 8, 16, 19, 23-25, 29, 31-32, 37-40, 43-45
Missionary Ridge, 44

Newton, John, Maj. Gen., 19

Ohio Battery, 37

Petersburg, VA, 24
Pickett, George E., Maj. Gen., 43-44

Rappahannock River, 27
Reynolds, John F., Maj. Gen., 9, 18
Richardson, L.J., Lieut., 24
Rickett, R. Bruce, Capt., 27, 29
Rock Creek, 18, 21-23, 25

St. Lawrence County, NY, 24
Salem, 1st Lieut., 27
Savage Station, 36
Schimmelfennig, Alexander, Brig. Gen., 9-10
Schurz, Carl, Maj. Gen., 9-10, 13, 15, 18, 39-40
Second Corps, 27
Seminary Ridge, 10, 18, 31, 39-40, 42-43
Sheridan, Philip, H., Maj. Gen., 44
Sherman, William T., Maj. Gen., 44
Sickles, Daniel E., Maj. Gen., 23-25
Slocum, Henry W., Maj. Gen., 22-23, 25
Steinwehr, Adolph von, Brig. Gen., 10, 13, 15, 18
Stuart, J.E.B., Maj. Gen., 8
Sumner, Edwin V., Maj. Gen., 36
Sykes, George, Maj. Gen., 23

Third Corps, 23
Troop Strengths, Union and Confederate, 8
Twelfth Corps, 22, 25

Wadsworth, Craig W., Capt., 38
Wainwright, Charles S., Col., 15
Washington, DC, 8
Wheatfield, 24
Wheeler, William, Lieut., 7, 10, 13, 15
Wiedrich, Michael, Capt., 7, 10, 27, 29, 40
Wilderness, 24
Wilkeson, Bayard, Lieut., 7, 10, 13
Williamsport, MD, 45
Winslow, George B., Capt., 24